Senior Sponsoring Editor: Katharine Glynn
Executive Marketing Manager: Roxanne McCarley
Project Manager: Rebecca Gilpin
Project Coordination, Text Design, and Electronic Page Makeup: PreMediaGlobal, Inc.

Cover Designer/Manager: Wendy Ann Fredericks
Senior Manufacturing Buyer: Dennis J. Para
Printer/Binder: R.R. Donnelley
Cover Printer: Lehigh Phoenix Color

Copyright © 2015 by Pearson Education, Inc.

PEARSON

www.pearsonhighered.com

Student ISBN 10:   0-321-95348-7
Student ISBN 13: 978-0-321-95348-3

...as helped thousands of students over nearly two decades, and like its counterpart, ...ers an alternative to lengthy, expensive, and often confusing style manuals. The distinguish- ...this text is that it isolates the skills related to research writing and moves students through a series ...ing activities that provide practice and reinforcement. The style manuals of professional organizations, such as the Modern Language Association (MLA) and the American Psychological Association (APA), and countless English handbooks provide explanations and examples of the conventions of documentation. They are valuable reference resources, especially for advanced writers. But for students in beginning writing classes, such books share a common weakness; they lack activity sections or practice sets that help in mastering the research writing task.

Beginning writers who face the complex demands of research writing need more than explanation and examples— they need practice. The best practice, of course, is in the context of personal writing and research. Unfortunately, such practice is often limited to one or two long papers (or a few short papers) per term, not enough to master all the stylistic options and conventions associated with the use of source material. Consequently, students often are left to struggle through years of college without ever completely understanding research writing even with a reference handbook at their side. *Research Writing Simplified* goes beyond explanations and examples to offer focused, sequenced *practice* in those conventions.

Research Writing Simplified is a concise yet thorough text that fits easily into various teaching approaches. Most composition teachers will want to use some of the exercises for in-class instruction, assigning others as homework. In classes where instructors spend less time on the conventions of documentation (perhaps in writing-across-the-curriculum courses), students can use the text as a self-teaching guide because the answers to Self-Tests and selected exercises are also provided in the book.

An **Instructor's Manual and complete answer key** are available online for instructors. Ask your Pearson sales representative, or go to http://www.pearsonhighered.com/educator for access.

What's New in This Edition

This eighth edition has been updated to reflect the electronic revolution taking place in research, including the most current guidelines from MLA, APA, and CMS. In the Controlled Source Research section we provide excerpts of articles related to the topic of "Life in Contemporary Society." It is a way for students to practice using research without having to find the sources themselves, and it also gives instructors control over the source material to better identify problems in its use. To promote more student focus on details of MLA/APA citations we have added exercises on punctuation.

We wish to thank our students and colleagues who helped in the preparation of the eighth edition and reviewers Kate Cottle, Wilmington University; Devon C. Holmes, University of San Francisco; Angie Macri, Pulaski Technical College; and Fredel Wiant, University of San Francisco. We are grateful also to Rebecca Gilpin, Katharine Glynn, and the production staff at Pearson for their help with this project.

Raymond H. Clines, *Jacksonville University*
Elizabeth R. Cobb, *Florida Gateway College*

R-1 Choosing a Topic

Being an *author* means being an *authority*. Sometimes our authority will come from personal experience, and sometimes it will come from reading, research, and careful thinking. Being an author also means being *authentic*, that is, presenting our ideas with an honest and genuine commitment to the topic itself and not merely for the sake of completing an assignment. Usually we do not do things very well unless we are sincerely motivated to do them, and this seems to be especially true with writing. In deciding on a topic it is important to find something of interest and significance to us. When the topic is assigned, we will write better if we see it as relevant to our lives in some way. Without a personal stake in a topic or a commitment to the ideas of our writing, we are doing little more than following instructions, and our purpose for writing may be inauthentic, for example, to please a teacher or to get a reasonable grade. To find your best topics, always look for ways to make the writing relevant to your own life.

Good writing consists of two equally important elements: a *thesis* and an *authentic purpose*. The *thesis* is what you hope your readers will learn from your writing. It is the public issue or point of the writing. The *purpose*, if it is authentic, is the reason the topic is important or interesting to you. Your thesis connects your topic to the reader, and an authentic purpose will connect you to your topic. Good writing exists at the intersection of our personal lives and the public world. In choosing a topic we need to consider two types of knowledge: knowledge of the self and knowledge of the world.

Knowledge of the Self. We need to consider what we already know, think, or care about. This knowledge is the basis of all good writing because it is here that we are the most *authentic* and *authoritative*—essential prerequisites for being an author. The best writing starts inside ourselves with an issue of significance to us and works outward toward a public issue that will be of interest to others. So in choosing a topic, the first place we need to explore is inside ourselves—our own passions and interests. What are the things you care most deeply about in life? What are the things you know most about? What life experiences have you had? We need to explore and respect that knowledge.

Knowledge of the World. Although good writing begins with a strong personal connection to a topic, there must also be a public dimension—some way to connect the readers to the topic. Our personal experiences and interests may have limited value to a general audience; therefore, they need to be enriched by knowledge *outside* ourselves. How can our personal interests be used to instruct or persuade other people? How are our personal experiences similar to and different from others' experiences, and how are they influenced by outside issues being debated in the public sphere?

As we begin making connections between public issues and our own lives, we will enrich our learning and we will express through our writing, not only a thesis, but also an authentic purpose with a unique and authentic voice.

Sometimes instructors will want you to write about topics related to specific readings and class discussion—topics with which you may not have a personal connection. There is nothing harder than trying to write about a subject you know little about and for which you care even less. If this happens, what can you do? Assigned topics may seem limiting at first, but they always offer plenty of room for individual expression to the student with imagination and determination.

To succeed as a writer you must push yourself to link whatever public issue you may be assigned to your own personal experiences or interests. In other words, how can you relate the topic to your own life? Where does your life intersect with it? If a history professor asks you to do research on a famous person in history, don't pick someone at random. Find a historical figure, even a minor one, who has had a direct impact on your life in some way, and discuss that impact in your paper. If a teacher assigns a poem, short story, or other work of literature, begin your writing with the place in the work that matters to you, and then move outward toward a public, reader-oriented significance. Writing about Shakespeare's *Macbeth*, for example, can be far more rewarding if you discuss the play in terms of personal motives or emotions you may have had, such as ambition, fear, or overconfidence. Identifying a common human experience in a literary work can produce excellent writing. In section SP-1, Sample Student Research Paper, notice how the student has taken the broad, impersonal topic of health care and personalized it with details from her own life. At the same time she has developed a public thesis her readers would find informative.

R-2 Researching a Topic

Probably as a result of experiences beginning in the early grades, many students mistakenly think that a research paper is a "report." Often students are told to research topics they are unfamiliar with and about which they have little to say: broad topics such as the golden age of Greek culture, the United States space program, or the causes of the Civil War. Such research involves little more than paraphrasing information from another source—often an encyclopedia or web site.

The kind of research expected in college, and later in professional life, goes beyond that required for mere "report" writing. Genuine research takes existing information and uses it to *advance* knowledge and create new insights from it, not merely report on it. For example, business executives may conduct marketing research to enable them to anticipate economic conditions unique to their business, whether it is making computers or making pizzas. Lawyers may conduct research to present cases involving issues as varied as pollution, divorce, or murder. In science, research is carried out to advance medical treatments, develop new drugs, predict earthquakes, or increase agricultural production. In college, good research writing involves *advancing* knowledge, coming up with original conclusions about a topic. Unless there is something new to be said about the subject, why write about it? Unless there is something *you* want to say, some unique and original insights that *you* want to share, your research will be little more than a "report" like those written by younger students.

In college research you will be expected to use a wide range of sources, such as professional journal articles, government documents, Internet sites, or interviews conducted in person, over e-mail, or at online newsgroups. Using a variety of sources will help you to understand the numerous sides to an issue and allow you to develop your own hypothesis or conclusion. After carefully evaluating your sources and weeding out dated, irrelevant, and biased information, you should use credible source information to advance an arguable thesis or assertion *of your own*. Your job is to present your ideas and the ideas of others in a responsible manner, using accurate and complete documentation. To give you an idea of what college-level research papers require, look at the sample research paper in sections SP-1 and SP-2.

Writing a research paper can be one of the most valuable learning experiences of any college course. More than any other activity, writing helps us to internalize what we learn. What you write about you make your own and you remember—long after you have forgotten the lectures or the reading material.

In college, research tends to proceed in an overlapping and recursive manner; however, there are distinct steps involved:

1. Familiarize yourself with the library and the various online databases and electronic sources available to you.

2. Select a subject you care about and that is appropriate to your assignment. Be able to answer the question "Why is this subject important to me?"

3. Check the *Library of Congress Subject Headings* or encyclopedia indexes to identify appropriate keywords. Without appropriate search terms your research may be limited or unsuccessful altogether.

4. Explore articles in general information sources such as encyclopedias or newspapers to become familiar with important names, dates, and the overall scope of your subject.

5. Move from general information sources to specific articles in periodicals and specialized journals. Continue reading and taking notes.

6. Form a tentative thesis: What is the main point you want your readers to get? What unique, fresh perspective can you give to the topic?

7. Continue reading. Revise and refocus your thesis as necessary.

8. Develop a plan and general outline for writing the paper.

9. Write a first draft and, if possible, get feedback on it.

10. Revise your draft and get more feedback from peers or your instructor.

11. Write a final draft and prepare a Works Cited or References list.

USING COMPUTER RESOURCES

Research has undergone vast changes in recent years, largely because of computer technology and the Internet. A great deal of information that was previously available only in books, periodicals, or newspapers is now available online through databases or the World Wide Web, and more is being added every day. Just a few years ago most research needed to be conducted in libraries, but that is not the case today. The ability to navigate the intricacies of computer information is becoming an essential skill for everyone because of its relevance to all areas of life, from academic subjects to commercial markets to personal entertainment. With keyword searches and Boolean logic, computers have the ability to sort through information for you, locating exactly what is relevant to your specific interests and making research much faster and easier.

Databases

Electronic databases collect and index information available in print, and these electronic collections can be immense. Even small academic libraries can be transformed into "world-class" research sites by subscribing to electronic databases. Databases are either portable or online. Portable databases are similar to books in that they can be purchased and carried

Figure R-1.1
EBSCOhost Site

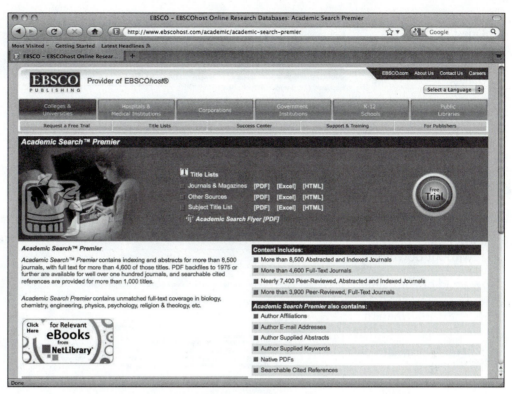

Reproduced with permission of EBSCO Publishing, Inc.

around. Compact discs with powerful storage capacities (CD-ROMs) are the most common type of portable databases, although libraries often have diskettes and magnetic tapes as well. Two examples of CD-ROM databases are *Academic Abstracts* and *PsychLit*. The latter indexes more than thirteen hundred journals in twenty-seven languages from about fifty countries.

Unlike portable databases, online databases are usually stored in large computers and made available through a type of subscription service accessed via phone lines. Information in these databases can be updated continually and may change without notice. Libraries often have online databases for the holdings in other libraries in the state, as well as their own. Online databases are even more powerful than portable databases. For example, *EBSCOhost* indexes more than 3,100 periodicals with more than three million articles, often including the entire text. (See Figure R-1.1.) *Ebsco Academic Search Complete* is even more comprehensive, with more than 5,300 full-text periodicals. *FirstSearch* indexes more than 16,000 journals in all subject areas.

In addition to listing titles and authors, both online and portable databases give abstracts or summaries of articles, making it much easier to determine whether a work is pertinent to your research. (See Figure R-1.2.)

The advantage of using a computer database is obvious when you compare it to the commonly used print index, the *Readers' Guide to Periodical Literature*, which indexes fewer than 200 magazines, does not provide abstracts of the articles, and is bound in yearly volumes. To conduct a search that goes back even a few years, you must look in each of the yearly bound volumes, in effect conducting several separate searches. Also, by using keywords you can conduct a search in many more ways than you can with print indexes, broadening and narrowing the search and thoroughly exploring all possible resources.

Computer databases are powerful research tools, but they do have limitations. Regardless of how sophisticated the computer databases at your library may be, it is still important to be familiar with print resources. Some disciplines are more timeless and book-driven, and current or updated information is not so important. Disciplines such as literature, history, and philosophy depend heavily on material written decades and even centuries ago. Research that requires information going back many years is probably best conducted through printed materials because database indexes tend to include only more recent information. Also in-depth research may involve little-known journals and local sources that are omitted from general database indexes and available only in print. Another limitation to computers is the lack of uniformity among systems. Print material will be the same in all libraries, but different libraries use different databases, and learning the various systems of

Figure R-1.2
ProQuest Results List

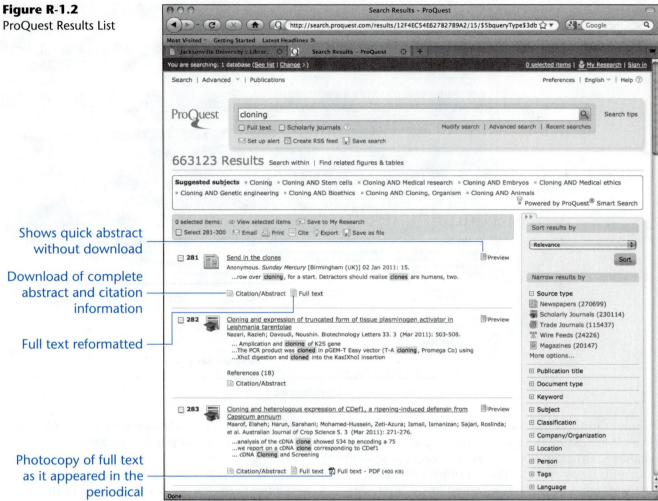

Shows quick abstract without download

Download of complete abstract and citation information

Full text reformatted

Photocopy of full text as it appeared in the periodical

The screen shots and their contents are published with permission of ProQuest LLC.

different libraries initially can be frustrating. Finally, when the library's computer system is down, print resources are always available so that you need not stop the research process to wait for the computer system to come online again. Librarians can assist as you learn the unique resources of a library, and they can help you locate other specialized materials as well, so describe your project to them early on.

The Internet

The Internet must be seen as one of the most significant technological advances of our time, and, like other major inventions—telephones, televisions, automobiles—it is reshaping our entire society. The Internet began in the 1960s as a way for the Defense Department to link computers in different parts of the country. It soon expanded to include computers at research institutions and universities, but the process of communicating and sharing information was difficult

to use. It wasn't until the 1990s, with the creation of the World Wide Web, that the Internet became practical for colleges, businesses, and individuals to use. Currently, the Internet is a global system of interconnected computer networks both large and small. Small networks, like those in universities, have their own systems. Large networks, such as World Wide Web, Telnet, Gopher, e-mail, Usenet, and FTP, are distinct online worlds in themselves; however, because each network has agreed to use the same protocols for communication, a vast "net" of interconnected computer systems has been created. The result is an electronic information and communication system that no one owns but to which anyone with a computer and modem can contribute. The democratic nature of the Internet is both its strength and weakness.

Wikipedia is a good example of the power of the Internet. It is a free encyclopedia collaboratively written by volunteers from all around the world. It currently has more than ten million articles in more than

Figure R-1.3
World Wide Web
Virtual Library

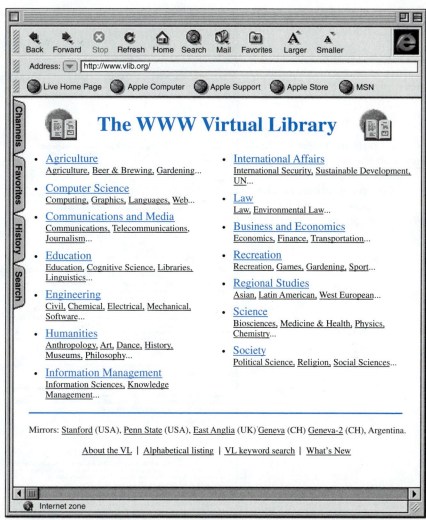

250 languages. Anyone with access to the Internet can contribute, but this can limit its value as a serious research tool. *Articles are not necessarily reviewed by experts, and users need to be aware that articles can contain false or debatable information.* However, inaccuracies are eventually corrected by the sheer number of people reading and editing it. Information is updated within minutes of events happening, and this can be an advantage over print encyclopedias.

Virtual libraries are a good place to begin a general search on the Internet, especially if you have not narrowed the topic. You can access the World Wide Web Virtual Library, which is organized much like a subject directory. (See Figure R-1.3) For academic research the best search engines are those that have been reviewed by librarians, such as the *Librarians' Internet Index.* Although many search engines attempt to organize hits in descending order

of relevance and credibility, library-edited indexes weed out sources; you may get fewer hits, but the ones you get almost always list authors and dates. Library-reviewed search engines allow you to move directly to more credible sites, avoiding the step of sorting through the less-reliable sources in a large index such as *Google.* However, *Google* now offers specialized advanced searches that compare to those of library-reviewed search engines. *Google Scholar* sorts peer-reviewed articles in the same way researchers do, based on the reputation of the author and the publication. (See Figure R-1.4.)

Many college-library home pages provide links to search engines. To save time later, use the "hot list" or "bookmark" feature to add helpful documents to your personal list of useful Internet addresses. You can narrow your search by employing the basics of keyword searching.

Figure R-1.4
Google Scholar

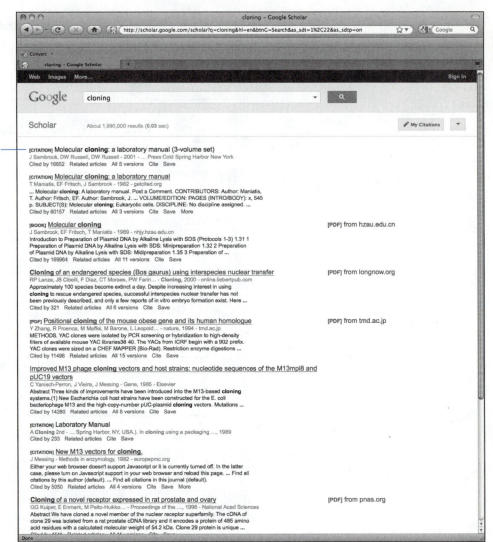

Sorts peer-reviewed articles based on the reputation of the author and the publication. Complete articles can be located through your library or on the web.

Keyword Searches

Beginning researchers often become frustrated with keyword searches. Without appropriate keywords, you may have limited success finding relevant articles. It is not enough to have a subject or topic; you must know *what the subject is called by other writers and academics.* Keep in mind that a particular topic can be identified by many different words or terms, and gaining some familiarity with them can make your research more efficient and focused. Experienced researchers rely on the *Library of Congress Subject Headings* index, which is available in the reference section of your library. In this index a general topic such as *advertising*, for example, has more than seventy terms, some broader (*business, retail trade, marketing*) and some narrower

(*commercial art, coupons, packaging, slogans, Internet advertising, psychology in advertising*). This index also lists related terms such as *propaganda, publicity,* and *public relations.* You can also talk to your classmates and professors and take note of the words they use when discussing your topic. A few minutes spent in the early stages talking with others, identifying the correct keywords, and focusing your topic can save many hours of random, haphazard research.

You can also find keywords by consulting the index of either an online or print encyclopedia. Every time you retrieve an article or book from a database or your library's online catalog, you will find related terms and subjects listed with the source information. (See Figure R-1.5.) Another way to improve your chances of finding relevant source material is to use

Figure R-1.5
Sample Online
Library Catalog Entry

Indicates *Library of Congress Subject Headings.* A good place to find additional keywords and terms for a topic.

Reproduced with permission of Jacksonville University.

advanced search strategies. Some version of Boolean operators, for example, is available on most search engines and databases. Boolean operators (AND, OR, NOT, +, −) allow you to broaden or narrow your search by combining and limiting keywords. The following examples illustrate the use of these terms in a keyword search:

- If you enter "millennium AND computers" the search will narrow to include only sources with both words in the text.
- If you enter "millennium OR computers" the search will broaden to include sources that have either of the words in the text.
- If you enter "millennium NOT computers" the search will find sources only on "millennium" that are not about computers.

You may notice that when you begin reading information from a particular site, certain words or phrases will be highlighted or underlined in a different color. These are "hot spots," which provide links to related topics when you click on them and can be another way to identify keywords and related terms.

You can also limit or expand your search by entering specific dates. You might begin by limiting your search to articles published in the past six months and then expand the search if too few articles are found.

Other areas to search are listservs and newsgroups. Listservs are mailing lists that allow e-mail to be sent to subscribers, people who share an interest in the focus of the listserv. To find a useful listserv for your own project, search <http://www.livinginternet.com>. Newsgroups, like listservs, are sites you can visit to enter or hear discussions on specific topics. To access them you would enter the appropriate URL. A good place to begin is by searching a complete index of newsgroups at Google-Public News Servers or Yahoo-Public Usenet Sites. Keep in mind that listservs and newsgroups are often best used to get a sense of the different issues; they may not be completely reliable for research purposes.

EVALUATING SOURCES

Because anyone can set up an information site on the Internet, evaluating sources is especially important. Obviously, sources such as the *New York Times* or *National Geographic* will be as credible as their print counterparts, as are reports from most agencies in the federal government. Likewise, growing

ONLINE RESOURCES

Help

Help with Writing:
 Purdue Online Writing Lab

Usenet Postings:
 <www.groupsgoogle.com>

Newsgroup Index:
 Google-Public News Servers or Yahoo-Public Usenet Sites

Directory of Online Journals and Periodicals:
 Google-Online Journals

American Psychological Association (APA) Documentation

Modern Language Association (MLA) Documentation

References

Information Please Almanac (includes *Random House, Webster's Dictionary,* and the *Columbia Encyclopedia*)

World Wide Web Virtual Library

Internet Public Library

Librarians' Index to the Internet

Britannica Online

Encarta Online Encyclopedia

News

New York Times

Washington Post

USA Today

Wall Street Journal

CNN

Magazines

Time

National Geographic

Wired

The New Yorker

Smithsonian

Government

Legislative Information:
 <http//thomas.loc.gov/>

Government Printing Office:
 <http//www.access.gpo.gov>

---

numbers of scholarly journals, both electronic and print, are available online. You can find a directory of online journals and periodicals at Google-Online Journals. Some Internet sites will be of little value because they are maintained by individuals, organizations, or businesses that have definite biases. At present, the Internet is not nearly as reliable as print sources or databases that reference print sources, because printed information is usually edited or reviewed by authorities in the field prior to publishing. Although many Internet sites do screen and edit their postings, no review process is *required* for Internet sites.

Here are some points to consider in determining the reliability of Internet sources:

- **Authority:** Who is the author? What qualifications are provided? Can the author be verified? Unless the individual or organization is identified, the source should not be used.
- **Accuracy:** Are the facts accurate? Is there an editor or peer review process? Are there links to known authorities? Is the information primary or secondary? That is, is the information coming firsthand from the person who did

the research or is it from someone reporting on another's research? The further away from primary sources you get, the less reliable the source becomes.
- **Objectivity:** Does the author have a bias, a personal ax to grind? Is the site affiliated with an educational institution as a research tool for academics (if so, ".edu" will appear in the address), or is it merely a web page? If the site is sponsored by a commercial business (.com) or an organization (.org), it should be evaluated for possible bias because it could be nothing more than a form of advertising or promotion. Government sites (.gov) are generally reliable.
- **Timeliness:** Is the site a "zombie"? Has it been updated recently, or is it one of the "walking dead"?

For more guidance on evaluating sources, see section R-4 Taking Notes and Outlining.

USING THE LIBRARY AND PRINT RESOURCES

There is very little in print that is not available in some form through the Internet, including books,

EVALUATING INTERNET SOURCES

- Check purpose of Internet sites. They should inform or explain. Choose ".edu," ".org," or ".gov" sites.
- Find author's qualifications to verify his or her credibility.
- Look for a recent update to the site.

- Information presented should be supported in a reputable manner with proper documentation.
- Information should be clearly organized and any links suggested by author of site should be accessible.
- Verify the site's overall professional "look." Beware of glitzy, flashy sites with links to commercial sites.

journals, magazines, and newspapers; however, many of these publications require a subscription. The resources in libraries are free and there are advantages to having physical copies in hand while doing research. In addition librarians are available to help with your search whether it is with the library holdings or online sources. For that reason physical libraries continue to be rich resources for any serious student. Most libraries have electronic indexing and searching tools that make finding library sources much easier. Often a single search at a library computer station will provide you with various resources—from books and periodicals to maps and atlases to audio and visual material. Books, of course, contain valuable information, but it is important to realize that magazine, journal, and newspaper articles contain more up-to-date information. It takes many months, even years, to write, publish, and eventually shelve books in a library or make them available online. Articles in weekly magazines such as *Newsweek* or *Time* discuss events that may have occurred as recently as last week. Books do have the advantage of offering in-depth discussions on topics, however, and they often include bibliographies.

An important way to locate information published in books is through the *Essay and General Literature Index,* a quick way to find focused information on a topic. For example, suppose that you are interested only in specific legal issues relating to abortion. One approach is to look through all the entries in the computer catalog, trying to determine which books would be relevant. An easier way is to look up the topic in the *Essay and General Literature Index.* There you will find specific references to chapters or sections of books pertaining to your exact area of interest. Good research relies on both books and articles—books for depth of coverage and articles for currency of information.

Newspaper articles offer important information that can be easily located through resources such as

News Bank, which indexes news stories published in local and state newspapers. Libraries often have their own index for regional newspapers as well. For any type of research involving local events, these resources are essential. For national issues, you would want to refer to the *New York Times Index,* which has brief summaries of all stories published in the *New York Times. Facts on File* is another valuable reference that summarizes news events on an international level. Ask your librarian for assistance in locating any of these print reference works or their online equivalents. More specialized professional journals are another resource to consult in your research. Authors of journal articles engage in more technical discussions. They are less likely to misrepresent the ideas they introduce because they are not writing for a general audience. Therefore, these works can give your project a high degree of credibility. You should spend a good deal of time locating such sources, as they can lead you to better-documented, more objective information. Scholarly journals are indexed in such resources as the *Social Sciences Index* and the *Humanities Index.* You will find the following academic disciplines listed in the *Social Sciences Index:*

Anthropology	Medical science
Economics	Psychology
Education	Public administration
Environmental science	Sociology
Law and criminology	

The *Humanities Index* includes articles in the following disciplines:

Archaeology	History
Classical studies	Language and literature
Folklore	Literary and political criticism
Performing arts	Religion
Philosophy	Theology

These indexes cover a broad range of academic fields; each discipline also publishes its own index for specific content areas. Examples include the *Art Index,* the *Applied Science and Technology Index,* and the *Engineering Index.* Because entry formats for each index vary, consult the beginning of the index for instructions on its use as well as a guide to the abbreviations used in that volume.

As you use the library more often, you will become acquainted with its print periodical holdings. If your library does not carry a book or publication, you can request an interlibrary loan.

Through the interlibrary loan service you can access the resources of libraries across the country. To use this service, you will need to fill out a request form at the circulation desk or perhaps use an online request form. Because your library will actually borrow this publication from another library, it will take at least a couple of days to receive the information.

SELF-TEST

Write the letter of the correct answer or answers in the blank.

1. Keyword searches are more successful when the terms used are taken (a) from popular magazines, (b) from *Library of Congress Subject Headings.*

    1. _____

2. If your library does not have what you need, you can (a) search the library's database for holdings in other libraries, (b) request an interlibrary loan to receive books and articles on your topic.

    2. _____

3. You would most easily find articles on history in (a) the *Social Sciences Index,* (b) the *Humanities Index.*

    3. _____

4. Although computer databases are powerful research tools, (a) research in disciplines such as literature and philosophy should be conducted in print material, (b) research going back many years should be conducted in print material.

    4. _____

5. Computer databases (a) become outdated quickly, (b) are not the same in every library.

    5. _____

6. If you have trouble finding relevant articles in an online database, (a) you are not searching appropriate keywords, (b) the database does not have information on that topic.

    6. _____

7. You would find newspaper articles of local interest in (a) *News Bank,* (b) the *New York Times Index.*

    7. _____

8. Resources that provide the most reliable information on a topic are (a) journals, (b) newspapers, (c) magazines.

    8. _____

9. The best place to find general background information on your topic is in (a) database articles, (b) the reference section of the library.

    9. _____

10. In determining the reliability of an Internet source, you should ask, (a) Does the site show bias? (b) Is an author identified? (c) Does the site have interesting graphics that hold my attention? (d) Does the URL address include *.com, .org,* or *.edu?*

    10. _____

Note: Answers to self-tests and other selected exercises can be found in the answer key near the back of the book.

WRITING ASSIGNMENTS: LIBRARY WORK

1. Use the *New York Times Index* to find an article of interest published on the day you were born. Summarize it in a paragraph of eight to ten sentences.
2. Select a topic that interests you from the World Wide Web Virtual Library. In a five-minute, non-stop freewriting session, discuss your thoughts on the topic (in about 150 words).

3. A classmate has begun a computer search for her paper on advertising, and no useful entries were found. List five steps you would suggest that she take.
4. In a paragraph or two, explain the difference between a database such as *EBSCOhost* and a search engine such as *Google*. Give examples of the different types of sources each would retrieve and of a source both would retrieve.

R-3 Preparing a Bibliography and a Preliminary Thesis

From the very beginning of the research process it is essential that you keep a record of books, articles, and other resources that you consulted pertaining to your topic. Computer databases are becoming increasingly sophisticated in identifying and printing a list of possible resources for any topic. Often, you can assess the value of an article for your purposes by reading an abstract that many databases such as *ProQuest* or *EBSCOhost* provide. General reference works such as online or print encyclopedias often list important sources at the end of each entry, and nearly every book and article you find will mention additional works. Just glancing through the bibliographies of books and articles can give you valuable information. Which names reappear? What are the recurring issues? A handy reference work that experienced researchers use is the *Bibliographic Index: A Cumulative Bibliography of Bibliographies*. It will direct you to sources that have useful bibliographies already prepared for you.

The best way to make use of the various retrieval systems and valuable resources available in a library is to follow a step-by-step research procedure. First, use print and electronic reference works to define and narrow your topic. Next, consult print and electronic indexes and catalogs to find article and book titles. Finally, locate your sources electronically on the library shelves, on microfilm, or through interlibrary loan. You may wish to follow this schedule:

1. Visit the reference section of your library, or use electronic databases and the Internet to locate sources that will help you to gain general back-ground on your topic. Note keywords, phrases, and important dates. Most researchers begin with the *Library of Congress Subject Headings*, which gives the different headings under which material may be listed in various reference books or databases. It can also be helpful in focusing a general research topic and defining specific areas of research. Other helpful resources include

Dictionaries
Facts on File
Almanacs
General and specialized encyclopedias (in print or online)

2. Consult computer databases, print indexes, and computer catalogs to find relevant titles and locations of general works on your topic:

Computer databases such as *EBSCOhost, ProQuest, Academic Abstracts, Psychological Abstracts, ERIC, News Bank/Readex, Statistical Abstracts, National Trade Databank*
Online library catalogs
Online search engines such as *Google Scholar, Bartleby*.com, *Refdesk.com,* and *Yahoo*
Internet listservs, blogs, and newsgroups such as *Google Blog Search, Yahoo Groups, World Newspapers*
New York Times Index
News Bank
Readers' Guide to Periodical Literature

More specialized articles can be found in

Applied Science and Technology Index
Social Sciences Index
Humanities Index
Education Index

Indexes for specific disciplines (e.g., art, business, environment, computer science, music)

Bibliographies

Computer databases more specific to the topic, such as *Business Source Elite* (business), *CINAHL* (nursing and health sciences), *ERIC* (education)

Web sites

3. Finally, locate your sources on the library shelves, at internet sites, or through interlibrary loan. During this stage you will find

Books	Essays
Articles	Audiovisual information
Reviews	Government documents

You will read and take notes from these resources and formulate your stance based on what you learn from them.

You may want to make printouts or photocopies of the bibliographies you find or jot them down for later reference. Be sure to include the following information with the notes that you take from each source:

Books

Name of author, last name first
Title of book (underlined or italicized)
Place of publication
Publisher's name
Date of publication
Library call number

Articles

Name of author
Title of article (in quotation marks)
Title of journal, magazine, or newspaper
Volume number and date of publication
Page numbers on which the article appears

Electronic Sources

All of the above information when given
Publication medium and vendor's name for CD-ROM
Publication date of the database in addition to date of document
Date of access and URL (DOI if available for APA)
    Page or paragraph numbers if available
Any referencing information that would help you locate it again

If you find plenty of information on your subject, you know you will have enough material to pursue your project. Begin reading some of the articles and browsing through the books to get a feel for the different angles to your subject. Pay close attention to table of contents headings, read first and last sections, and skim indexes.

WRITING A THESIS

Once you have briefed yourself on the various issues and approaches to your subject, you are ready to develop a *preliminary thesis*, a statement that expresses your particular stance on your subject. As you continue your research you may need to change your thesis, but it is important to write one with care at this stage to help you focus your work. Four steps are involved in formulating a thesis:

1. A thesis states the objective of a paper in a single statement that identifies (1) the topic and (2) your position or assertion on the topic. In the examples that follow, notice that sentence **A** identifies a general topic, sentence **B** narrows or limits the general topic, and sentence **C** takes a position or makes an assertion.
   A. Reality television shows
   B. The popularity of reality television shows
   C. Reality television shows are popular because they give viewers the opportunity to see regular people in challenging situations. (topic + position = thesis)
   A. Computers
   B. The effects of computers on our lives
   C. Computer technology is transforming our ability to deal with complex issues. (topic + position = thesis)

2. A thesis does not make an announcement:

   The subject of this paper will be reality television shows.

   Computers and their effects on our culture will be the concerns of this essay.

   In this paper I will discuss the effects of computers on our culture.

3. A thesis avoids overly general, vague, or abstract wording. Keep your topic limited to an objective that is appropriate to the length and scope of your paper. For example, if your subject is music or terrorism, do not try to cover all aspects of the controversies surrounding music censorship or the threat of terrorism. Treat some important aspect of your subject in depth rather than giving the entire topic a cursory treatment. Because it is too broad, the following sentence says very little:

Providing for the homeless challenges America's largest cities.

This revised version is better. Notice how it mentions possible specific subpoints of the essay:

America's large cities should rehabilitate homeless people by providing them with shelter, food, and skills training.

4. A thesis contains only one main idea. Although it is acceptable and even advisable to mention specific subpoints in a thesis statement, be sure the thesis focuses on only one main idea. Notice how the following sentences appear to have two separate ideas:

America's large cities should rehabilitate homeless people by providing them with skills training and people should be more tolerant of them.

Many people find computer technology baffling, but it is transforming our ability to deal with complex issues.

Reality television shows are popular because regular people are put in challenging situations and advertisers are cashing in.

Formulating a preliminary thesis and compiling a preliminary bibliography will allow you to proceed to the next step in the process: taking notes.

SELF-TEST

In the blank, write the letter that indicates the stage of the research process during which you would most likely consult each listed source.

(a) Definition and overview of the subject
(b) Identification of potential sources
(c) Reading and viewing specific sources

1. *Facts on File*   1. _____
2. A book titled *The Marcos Dynasty*   2. _____
3. Abstracts of English studies   3. _____
4. The Free Internet Encyclopedia   4. _____
5. The *General Science Index*   5. _____
6. An online computer database with information on holdings in other libraries   6. _____
7. *Webster's Third New International Dictionary*   7. _____
8. A *New York Times* article on pit bull terrier attacks   8. _____
9. www.expandinglight.org   9. _____
10. *Dissertation Abstracts International*   10. _____

In the blank, write the letter of the phrase that describes each thesis statement.

(a) An arguable (successful) thesis statement
(b) An announcement
(c) An overly general thesis or statement of fact without a position
(d) A thesis containing more than one main idea

11. Automobile accidents have killed more people than major world wars.   11. _____
12. Tattoos give teenagers a way to rebel against parental values, and they are very difficult to have removed.   12. _____
13. Children of divorced parents are often forced to take on adult responsibilities sooner and mature faster.   13. _____
14. This paper will explore the problems faced by gay and lesbian adolescents.   14. _____
15. Terrorism is an evil force in today's world.   15. _____

WRITING ASSIGNMENTS: LIBRARY WORK

1. Compile a preliminary bibliography for a topic that interests you or one selected from the list that follows. Try to find at least four sources, including a specialized journal. After you have read some of the articles, compose a preliminary thesis statement for a five-page research paper. Possible topics:

dysfunctional families   cat ownership
hang gliding   day care options
environmental concerns

2. In one paragraph, predict the steps involved in continuing the research and writing process for the subject you chose for Writing Assignment 1.

R-4 Taking Notes and Outlining

All source material must be evaluated before it can be used in research. Often the evaluation will take place immediately, as you glance at irrelevant titles or old publication dates. Sometimes you must skim through a source, paying particular attention to the table of contents, chapter headings, introductions, and summaries. All source materials, print and electronic, should be assessed on the basis of four criteria: relevance, currency, credibility, and objectivity.

1. **Relevance:** Your preliminary thesis will serve as a guide to determining the relevance of sources—which is why it is always a good idea to write one. By giving your research a clear focus from the beginning, you can save yourself time and effort, especially if you have a tendency to get lost on the Web. For example, if you are investigating the emotional effects of cosmetic surgery, it is unlikely that articles on surgical procedures will be of much use.

2. **Currency:** Likewise, an article published in the current year detailing recent psychological findings in the area of cosmetic surgery would be more useful than a book published ten years ago. Whether the information is current or not is an important concern for most research topics. Some exceptions might include topics dealing with historical or literary focuses. Recent newspaper and magazine articles usually offer more up-to-date information than books.

3. **Credibility:** You will also want to consider the author's credibility during this source evaluation phase. Is the author respected by experts in the field? Has this author written other publications on this topic or related topics? The publication itself can be a key to assessing the credibility of a source. At one extreme are tabloids such as the

National Enquirer or a nonattributed home page on the Web, which no one takes seriously. At the other extreme are prestigious professional journals that will publish articles only after careful screening called peer review. However, these journals may be too technical or too difficult for the purpose of general research.

4. **Objectivity:** Many respected publications are aimed at specific audiences and have editorial policies that may affect the objectivity of articles published in them. The topic of music lyric censorship would be dealt with quite differently in *Rolling Stone* and in a chat room on the World Wide Web for Christian parents concerned about the morality of popular music. The issue of scientifically controlled births would be treated differently in the *Journal of Fermentation and Bioengineering* and in *Catholic Digest*. Even major newspapers are sometimes known for being conservative or liberal, pro-Democrat or pro-Republican. Thus, editorials from these newspapers may be convincing, but they may not present the whole picture. Also, after monitoring the discussions of online newsgroups, listservs, and chat rooms you can usually detect a bias. Only by looking at your topic from the perspectives presented in a number of different sources can you be sure of getting the complete story.

To illustrate the process of source evaluation, imagine that you are writing a research paper on the importance of educating Third World countries on the dangerous spread of AIDS. You begin to skim the sources you have gathered so far:

A 2013 federal government site at <www.aids .gov> that deals with HIV and AIDS research and politics

A September 2013 article titled "AIDS-associated Cryptococcosis in Bujumbura, Burundi: An Epidemiological Study," from the *Journal of Medical and Veterinary Mycology*

An August 2012 editorial titled "Help Is on the Way," which appeared in the *New York Times*

A 1990 sex education pamphlet published by the state of Maryland

A November 2009 *Readers' Digest* narrative titled "Meeting with the Grief in Rural Costa Rica," written by a Christian missionary

A December 16, 2010, *New York Times on the Web* article titled "Africa's Culture of Mourning Altered by AIDS Epidemic"

You could conceivably use information from most of these sources. The federal government site might prove useful during the beginning stages of research for general background as you define and characterize the scope of the problem. The *Readers' Digest* and *New York Times on the Web* articles might help you to personalize the description of the disease's effects on victims and families. In the body of your paper you will want to rely on authoritative sources such as the article from the *Journal of Medical and Veterinary Mycology*. In your conclusion you could present some of the solutions offered by the *New York Times* editorial, "Help Is on the Way." Do not be reluctant to discard sources that are not relevant, current, credible, or objective—such as the sex education pamphlet published prior to the outbreak of AIDS.

TAKING NOTES

Evaluating sources plays an important part in determining the articles from which you will want to take careful notes and on which you will want to spend less time. Each writer has a slightly different method of taking notes and recording source information. Some use word processors to summarize and paraphrase relevant source information, and some will highlight information from copies of articles obtained in the library or printed from the Internet. Whatever system you use, be sure to record the information and its source accurately. One practical system involves taking notes on note cards and writing down bibliographic information on separate note cards. Cards can easily be rearranged to fit your outline, whereas highlighted computer printouts or large sheets of paper bearing a variety of notes can lead to confusion as you try to work the notes into your paper. Cards measuring 4" × 6" give you more room to record your notes, and their size can distinguish them from your bibliography cards, which generally measure 3" × 5". It is not necessary to record all of the publication information on your note cards because that information is what you include on your bibliography cards. Just be sure to devise some way to identify the source of your notes (the author's last name will usually suffice), and *always include specific page numbers* because that information will not be on your bibliography card. Keep your bibliography cards nearby so that you can refer to them in identifying your sources. Here are a few additional tips on note taking:

- Record one idea per card, and write on only one side. That way, cards can be rearranged easily and important information will not be overlooked.
- Title each card with a brief description—a phrase—of what the note is about, but use full, well-developed sentences in the note itself. This will make it easier to arrange your notes and write your first draft later.
- Before beginning a new note-taking session, read over your last set of note cards to recall where you were in your thinking.

In addition, decide whether to summarize, paraphrase, or quote the source directly. Each of these methods of note taking will be discussed in detail in upcoming sections Most of your notes should be in the form of summaries or paraphrases, which means that they should be written *in your own words*. This step is essential to research writing because it forces you to think about and assimilate the material. Before you can summarize or paraphrase source material, you must understand it thoroughly. You can condense whole books or articles into summaries if you are interested only in the main ideas. Paraphrasing involves rewording source material without condensing it. When you put the information into your own words, it is important not to misrepresent the author or change the findings to suit the needs of your paper.

Writing a research paper means presenting your ideas and the ideas of others in your own personal way, so be selective about information that you decide to quote directly. A few select direct quotations can add emphasis, emotion, or authority to your paper, but too many will weaken a paper by causing you to lose credibility as the author of what you have written. Remember to put quotation marks around all exactly reproduced text as with summaries and paraphrases, be sure to note the author and page number.

When you want to record key phrases or important terms, you should take *key term* notes. These are useful when you are writing about topics that have unusual terminology; they can be a quick way to record important points, when a source is too general and not worth summarizing or paraphrasing. For example, an article on buying a house might produce the following key phrases: *title, escrow, seller, cash-out, lending company, mortgage, prime interest rate,* and *liens*.

As you take notes, you will become adept at distinguishing between fact and opinion. A fact can be proved; an opinion offers information that cannot be documented. For example, the statement "Humane Society officers found five puppies in a park Dumpster today" can be proved. By contrast, the statement "The five puppies found in the park Dumpster today were most likely left there by teenagers, who usually have no respect for animals" offers only a conjecture or a guess about the situation. It reveals the author's bias, but the statement itself cannot be proved.

You may wish to use both opinions and facts to support your thesis, but distinguish between these two types of information for your reader. For example, the statement that teenagers do not usually respect animals may support your thesis that adults unfairly blame crimes on teenagers. Make sure your reader knows that you are using an opinion, though. Be aware that reviews and editorials contain more opinion than fact.

When you get more practice at distinguishing between fact and opinion, you also learn to avoid jumping to incorrect conclusions. A helpful hint for avoiding premature judgments is to check dates of publication and make certain that you have enough current information to draw conclusions. For example, a pamphlet published by the Kentucky Department of Education in 1955 may advocate the use of corporal punishment by teachers in classrooms in some situations. More recent Department of Education reports recommend entirely different disciplinary procedures.

Here is another bit of advice: Try summarizing what you have read in one sentence before writing anything down. You might save yourself from writing too many notes. Also, give yourself some time to absorb your reading.

Finally, document everything that you use from outside sources. Consider the following tips:

- Always put quotation marks around directly quoted material.
- Always put source information on each note card or computer printout, including specific page numbers.
- When summarizing and paraphrasing, put the original passage out of sight before writing your own version.

If you take these tips too lightly, you may be on your way to the illegal practice of *plagiarism*—using another author's ideas as if they were your own. Lack of careful attention to documentation may cause you to commit plagiarism unintentionally. That is, you may forget to attribute information to a source, or you may forget to include a page number. Nonprint and print materials are protected by copyright laws. Neither civil courts nor academic communities tolerate plagiarism (intentional or unintentional), and in most institutions you will fail both the paper and the course for practicing it. Section C-3 provides a detailed discussion of plagiarism and ways to avoid it.

WORKING THESIS AND OUTLINE

As your note taking proceeds, you will fine-tune your preliminary thesis and develop a working outline. Writing a thesis and an outline can make the writing process much easier. They will guide your note taking by organizing the main points of your topic. They require more thought and planning than the scribbled lists you may have used successfully to organize shorter papers, but it is planning that will pay off when you begin writing the paper. Ideally, your thesis, outline, and note taking should change and evolve together as you complete your research. Remain open to new ideas all through the note-taking process, modifying the direction of your research, the thesis, and the outline to accommodate new information. Every time you come across a new bit of information (or fail to find what you need), ask yourself whether your thesis is still valid and whether your outline has been fine-tuned enough to guide the direction of your paper. Grappling with the complexities of an issue is the first step in genuine understanding, and that is what research is all about.

Shanna R. Chauncey, the writer of the sample research paper in sections SP-1 and SP-2, grappled with a couple of thesis statements before she was satisfied. In her preliminary research she gathered the following key terms and ideas: holistic medicine; integrated medicine; importance of scientific data; limitations of scientific approach; reasons for seeking alternative therapies; and escalating medical costs. She began with a statement that she later criticized as too broad and biased:

Overall, alternative medical practitioners practice safer, more cost-effective, and more humane medicine than do mainstream doctors.

From her initial reading, she decided that actually the trend in medicine was not so focused on separating the approaches into two camps. She revised her thesis to read:

The question is no longer whether or when the medical community will accept alternative medicine but how they should integrate it.

This statement also suffered from being too broad, and it was not arguable. More reading and ruminating led to the final thesis statement found in the sample research papers in sections SP-1 and SP-2.

The time has come for practitioners to include alternative therapies in their treatment plans because alternative medicine addresses the public's desire for holistic care, prevention, and guidance in how to establish a healthy lifestyle.

PREPARING A DETAILED OUTLINE

An outline allows you to fine-tune and organize your ideas, which can be the most difficult part of writing your paper. First look through your notes to determine the major topics that will support your thesis, including the placement of quotations and references. If you used note cards, you may just begin sorting them into idea piles. If you took notes or wrote preliminary drafts on notebook paper, you can employ this same process by cutting out sections with scissors and sorting by main ideas into piles. If you kept your notes in a computer file you could cut and paste them by topic into smaller files. For example, in the sample outline that follows, the writer, Shanna Chauncey, divided her outline into four major topics to support her thesis: Medical practitioners must recognize the importance of alternative medicine in order to meet the needs and desires of their patients. She used a full-sentence outline and simply stated four points:

1. Traditional medicine must acknowledge the importance of holistic care.
2. Holistic care focuses on prevention rather than emergency care.
3. Lifestyle changes are often required in alternative medical care.
4. The public's interest in alternative medicine is growing.

Once she determined these major points, she decided how to order them to make her case most effectively. Most writers opt for arranging information from least important to most important, as readers are more likely to remember what they read last. She then broke down her major points into supporting subtopics, which became the focus of her paragraphs. The sample paper in section SP-1 shows how each subtopic is developed in paragraph form.

In the process of determining the major divisions of your subject, you may find yourself discarding notes that don't seem to support your thesis or that don't have enough information on a particular subtopic to warrant their use. You can certainly use briefer phrasing, but the value of using full sentences is that you have essentially begun writing your paper. Although an outline can provide a solid place to begin, more ideas will occur to you in the process of writing your first draft and a different organization may emerge. Your learning experience is not complete until you have written the final draft.

SAMPLE OUTLINE FOR STUDENT RESEARCH PAPER

Chauncey i

Outline

<u>Thesis Statement:</u> The time has come for conventional practitioners to include alternative therapies in their treatment plans because alternative medicine addresses the public's desire for holistic care, prevention, and guidance in how to establish a healthy lifestyle.

<u>Introduction:</u> Explanation of the conventional approach to medicine I experienced during my childhood as a doctor's daughter and the parallels of my interest in alternative medicine with the public's current exploration of alternative therapies. (Use Eisenberg statistics.)

I. The importance of medical practitioners' acknowledgment of the holistic approach to health care.
   A. Description of typical visit to conventional doctor.
   B. Description of typical visit to an alternative practitioner.
   C. The body systems must be viewed as interdependent.
      (Use Goldberg quote: "Intrinsic interrelatedness. . . .")
      (Use Weil quote: "Most of the treatments. . . .")
      (Use Harris quote with Figure 1, "Chakras.")

II. Prevention plays an integral role in alternative approaches whereas conventional medicine focuses on emergency care.

   A. Description of my own experience with medical doctors regarding my back problem.
     (Use Hoey quote: "Any illness that we label. . . .")

   B. Comparison of experience with massage therapist in the treatment of my back problem.

   C. Discussion of other preventive approaches.
     (Use Goldberg idea about the need for conventional doctors to get away from "rescue" medicine.)

III. In order for alternative medicine to become a part of health care, individuals must adopt lifestyle changes.

   A. Health care professionals must give back the responsibility for health to individuals.
     (Use Micozzi quote: "Health is something. . . .")

   B. Adopting a philosophy of health will help people to make the necessary dramatic changes toward taking control of their own health.

     1. Chinese medicine

     2. yoga

     3. Ayurvedic medicine

   C. A brief outline of two systems of health care from Dr. Whitaker and Dr. Chopra.

IV. It is time to pay attention to the public's overwhelming interest in alternative medicine.

   A. It is possible and desirable to integrate alternative and conventional medicine.
     (Use example of Dr. Weil's innovative program at University of Arizona.)

   B. Conclusion: Doctors may be more willing to commit to the integration of alternative medicine after they experience some of the benefits of nonconventional practices.

SELF-TEST

Indicate in the blank whether each statement is true (T) or false (F).

1. It's necessary to record author, title, and date of publication on each note card.   1. _____

2. You can assume that if something is in print or on a computer screen, it is a factual record of a topic.   2. _____

3. The best place to begin looking for the most recent sources on a topic is the electronic library catalog.   3. _____

4. You need to develop a system for note taking that works best for you.   4. _____

5. You should include your own opinions and reactions as you record summaries and paraphrases on note cards.   5. _____

6. It's not necessary to note the author and page numbers for key term notes.   6. _____

7. If you consult too many sources, you run the risk of jumping to conclusions.   7. _____

8. When you are prioritizing sources, you should give more weight to the more technical articles.   8. _____

9. Using many direct quotations in your paper will cause your readers to
lose interest and to suspect your credibility.   9._____

10. Paraphrasing helps you to develop your own ideas on a topic.   10._____

For each of the following, identify which type of note-taking skill you would
most likely use by placing the letter of the correct description in the blank.

    (a) direct quote
    (b) paraphrase
    (c) summary
    (d) key term

11. While listening in on an online newsgroup discussion, you come upon a
controversial but articulate statement by a respected individual regarding your topic.   11._____

12. An encyclopedia article discusses and defines general terms on your topic.   12._____

13. A textbook passage offers a long explanation of an important general idea
related to your topic.   13._____

14. An author elaborates on an idea that you would like to include in your paper.
You feel that you could relate it better in your own wording.   14._____

15. An author lends a particular emotion to an idea that you think you cannot
improve on.   15._____

Note: To check your answers, turn to the answer key near the back of the book.

WRITING ASSIGNMENTS: LIBRARY WORK

1. Use the following passage to practice writing
(a) a summary note card, (b) a paraphrase note
card, and (c) a direct quote note card. Use real
note cards, if possible, and remember to record the
proper documentation.

Source: Kennedy, Joyce Kutaka. "Student Empowerment
through On-Stage Theater." *Individual Psychology* 46.2
(2011): 184–86. Print.

Educators have tried numerous inventions to capture the
wandering attention of the modern child. Cooperative
learning techniques, math manipulatives, and a
"hands on" approach to science are but a few. These
approaches—which require active involvement of the student in his or her own learning process—are now emerg-
ing as a direction for the future of mainstream education.
Parents, administrators, and the teaching profession are
urging teachers to make education come alive for students
everywhere.

2. Find an article or a book of interest and make the
following types of note cards: (a) bibliography,
(b) summary, (c) paraphrase, and (d) direct quote.

C-1 Documentation Systems

Documenting the sources of information and wording taken from others is an essential part of writing research papers. For the sake of academic honesty, as well as copyright laws, you must let readers know which ideas are yours and which have come from other people. Readers must be able to locate your sources if they want to learn more about the subject or to verify your interpretation. In fact, you will undoubtedly want to track down some of the sources cited by authors in the articles and books you read. It is through such cross-referencing that a person becomes truly knowledgeable on a topic. A documentation system is merely a set of mechanical conventions that allows a writer to inform readers about sources.

Different fields of study have different systems of documentation to emphasize what is important in those disciplines. In the sciences and the social sciences, for example, information quickly becomes outdated; advances in knowledge are so rapid that identifying *when* a particular study was published is essential. Consequently, documentation systems in those disciplines—the Council of Science Editors (CSE), the American Psychological Association (APA), and the *Chicago Manual of Style (CMS)*—usually emphasize *names and dates:* (Wooferini, 2013, p. 7).

In the humanities, by contrast, the works of Mozart, Shakespeare, or Thomas Jefferson may have been written hundreds of years ago, but they are not considered outdated; thus, *who* wrote something is more important than *when* it was written. The Modern Language Association (MLA) documentation system emphasizes *names* only: (Jefferson 61). By using a particular documentation system, you are essentially acculturating yourself to the thinking of a specialized community of scholars. Different systems express information about sources in ways that complement the thinking of a particular discipline. In the beginning years of college, you can use the MLA system in most courses requiring research. As you advance in your study and begin taking upper-division courses in a declared major, instructors usually specify which system they require for their assignments. Be sure to clarify this point before you begin research projects.

C-2 In-Text Citations

In-text citations refer to the information about sources that is given in the narrative or text of a paper. There are two basic methods for providing in-text citations:

parenthetical and *numerical*. The most practical in-text citation system is the parenthetical system. Information is given in parentheses in the text and keyed to a list arranged alphabetically at the end: **(Crawford 112)** for MLA or **(Crawford, 2013, p. 112)** for APA. Information that is placed in parentheses must correspond to the information on the Works Cited or References page. Whatever word appears first in the left margin of the Works Cited or References list will be the signal word for in-text citation. Depending on the source, that signal word may be someone's last name, a sponsoring organization, or a title. If no author or sponsoring organization is provided, you can refer to the work using a shortened form of the article title in parentheses. If no page number is provided, as is often the case with electronic sources, you will have to omit this information. With minor variations in format, the parenthetical system is used by the APA and the MLA. The following is a typical example of a paraphrase in MLA style:

> **If all of the articles on *Wikipedia* were made into a book, it would be over 225 million pages long, or 13 miles thick, and would require a bookshelf the length of Manhattan Island in New York (Dalby 46).**

The parenthetical documentation—(Dalby 46)—indicates that the information in the sentence came from page 46 of an article by Dalby. By referring to the Works Cited list at the end of the paper, readers will find the complete bibliographic information. Notice that the page numbers listed for the article in the Works Cited list will be for the *entire* article while the page number in parentheses refers to the specific page.

> **Dalby, Eliza Jane. "The World and Wikipedia: How We Are Editing Reality." *Journal of Telecommunications* 15 Jan. 2013: 44–56. Print.**

The *Chicago Manual of Style* and the Council of Science Editors use numerical systems with footnotes or endnotes, where superscript numbers in the text are keyed to sources placed either at the bottom of the page or together at the end of the paper:

> **R. J. Vilenkin believes the universe began with many "big bangs."[3]**

Numbers can also be placed in the text in parentheses and keyed to references that are arranged at the end in the order they appear in the paper:

> **Our universe began from an explosive burst 13.82 billion years ago (6).**

> **6. Webb, B. "How Did the Universe Begin?" Sci. Amer. 2013, 275(4): 79–81.**

The sample research paper in *CMS* style on pages 72–74 gives more examples of the numerical system. It has become less popular because of several disadvantages. Placing separate footnotes at the bottom of a page presents problems for typesetters and increases publishers' costs. Even a number system that is keyed to a list of works at the end of the text has disadvantages. Once a manuscript is typed, additions or deletions to the sources cannot be made without changing both in-text citation numbers and the numbers for the works cited. Also, readers who may be interested in the authors being cited must turn to the source list each time a reference is given in the text.

ELECTRONIC SOURCES

Wikis, blogs, microblogs, podcasts, Twitter, YouTube, Facebook, personal email, government web sites (.gov), educational web sites (.edu), LinkedIn, My Space—the number of social networking and Internet sites grows more varied every day. Nearly anything in print, from newspapers and magazines to automobile owner's manuals, has an electronic version and often its own web site. When documenting electronic sources in the body of your paper, the same conventions are used as with print sources: **Your source information must correspond to the source information on the Works Cited or References page.** The first word or phrase that appears in the left margin of the Works Cited entry, whether it is someone's name, a sponsoring organization, or a title, will be the *required* citation. It can be worked into the text of your sentence or placed in parentheses (not both). Additional information about the source can be included in your paper as appropriate, but what you put in parentheses must follow style and punctuation conventions exactly.

> MLA: ("Wildlife at Risk" 28)
> "Wildlife at Risk from Climate Change." *National Wildlife* Oct./Nov. 2013: 28. Print.
>
> APA: (Wildlife at risk, 2013, p.28)
> Wildlife at risk from climate change. (2013, October/November). *National Wildlife*, p.28.

Often electronic sources do not have page numbers, in which case you will not cite any. If the author uses some other system, such as paragraph or section numbers, include these numbers in the body of your paper. (See section S-2, General Guidelines for Documenting Sources, #7.)

C-3 Avoiding Plagiarism

The first step in avoiding plagiarism is to have something that *you want to say* about a topic. Usually it will

be necessary to spend some time becoming familiar with a topic. As suggested in steps three and four of the research process (R-2), explore your topic from various angles on the Internet, in encyclopedias, and in general reference works. As you move from the background information in general reference works to specific articles, you will begin to see problems or questions that have not been answered and connections that have not been made—in short, you will begin to develop *your own ideas* about the topic, which then become the basis of your preliminary thesis.

As you work through the activities in this book, you will learn the steps of honest scholarship. First of all, be sure to set aside plenty of time to complete your research; it is in the area of time management that beginning researchers encounter the most trouble. Most writing involves a period of conscious and subconscious mental activity—an incubation period—before ideas begin to surface in original ways. It is crucial that you allow time for this process. By running yourself up against a clock, you leave yourself with fewer and fewer options. This leads to the most dangerous option of all: taking shortcuts that result in plagiarism.

Plagiarism is intentionally or unintentionally giving the impression that words or ideas from another source are your own. Plagiarism takes many forms. Occasionally students will submit papers written by other students, taken from fraternity or sorority files, or purchased from firms offering "term paper assistance." These days, ready-made papers can even be found on the Internet. Even resubmitting a paper that you wrote for another class may be perceived as ethically unsound. College students rarely copy entire articles from books, journals, or encyclopedias, but sometimes they intentionally copy passages verbatim or rephrase long sections of articles without acknowledging sources. What these students fail to realize is that experienced readers, such as college instructors, can invariably detect changes in prose style and levels of expertise on a topic. Even if such examples occur unintentionally because of careless note taking, severe penalties can be imposed. Of all the things that may detract from the quality of a piece of writing, plagiarism is the most serious fault. It is a form of intellectual and academic dishonesty. Research depends on the borrowing of material, but it is in the process of analyzing it, synthesizing it, and reshaping it into *your own perspective* that learning is advanced, both for yourself and for the academic community at large. Plagiarism defeats the whole purpose of your education and ultimately undermines the advancement of learning in the broadest sense. No college or university tolerates it, and most instructors will fail students who practice it. The issue of plagiarism is not confined to the academic community; state and federal laws impose severe fines and even imprisonment for stealing intellectual property.

COMMON KNOWLEDGE

One area that can be confusing to researchers involves the use of information classified as common knowledge. If a fact or an idea is well known or easily observable, it need not be documented if it is not taken verbatim from another source. Well-known proverbs or sayings need no citation. Students sometimes abuse this rule by claiming that any information they did not document was well known to them, but to be considered common knowledge, information must be well known to a general audience. Here are examples of statements and sayings considered common knowledge:

> Most teenagers long for the freedom to live on their own.
> Rush hour traffic in most cities is becoming worse each year.
> "Haste makes waste."
> "Well begun is half done."

Historical and geographic facts that are easily verified are also usually not documented. Here are examples of such facts:

> Theodore Roosevelt was the twenty-sixth president of the United States.
> Psychologist Carl Jung received his M.D. degree from the University of Basel in 1900.
> Of the fifty states, Wyoming ranks ninth in size (96,988 square miles) and fiftieth in population (550,000).

EXAMPLES OF PLAGIARISM

The following excerpt is from an article by William Ellis titled "Culture in Transition." Specific examples of how plagiarism can occur follow the excerpt.

Original: **World problems such as poverty, pollution, war, and hunger are inherent in the current system of world order based on nation-states and economic competition. They can be solved if people know and understand one another on a global, grass-roots basis. By developing people-to-people linkages irrespective of national borders, we can start to ameliorate global tensions and inequities.**

Word-for-Word Plagiarism Without Quotation Marks

Plagiarized (MLA): **William Ellis asserts that world problems such as poverty, pollution, war, and hunger are inherent in the current system of world order based on nation-states and economic competition (23).**

This is an example of the most blatant form of plagiarism. The first sentence of the original has been copied verbatim. Even though the source has been acknowledged, the writer must also include quotation marks around passages copied word for word. The writer gives the impression that the passage is a paraphrase when, in fact, it is a direct quotation.

Plagiarized (APA): **Ellis (2013) asserts that world problems such as poverty, pollution, war, and hunger are inherent in the "current system of world order based on nation-states and economic competition" (p. 23).**

WHAT MUST BE CITED

Citation is necessary for all types of intellectual property. Even common knowledge must be cited if you are using it verbatim or using the original sequence or organization of the ideas. The legal status of information has no bearing on whether it must be cited; that is, information that is not copyrighted or is in the public domain still needs citation.

WHEN TO CITE

If you are using someone's

- original words
- ideas that you summarize
- ideas that you paraphrase
- organization or sequence of ideas
- isolated fact
- interesting phrase
- unique word or term
- painting, sculpture, or photograph
- musical composition
- advertisement
- cartoon
- map or chart
- ideas from a speech or lecture
- ideas from an interview or conversation
- experiment
- ideas from video, film, or television program

The writer has partially corrected the problem of the first plagiarized example by placing quotation marks around some of the borrowed passage. The first part of the sentence is still word for word from the original. *All* material copied verbatim must be put in quotation marks and documented.

Patchwork Plagiarism

Plagiarized (MLA): **Global tensions and inequities can be solved if people begin to help one another on a grass-roots basis, moving beyond the current world order of economic competition (Ellis 23).**

The writer has completely reordered the information but continues to use much of the exact wording. "Global tensions and inequities," "grass-roots basis," "current world order," and "economic competition" are all taken verbatim from the original. Even with the reordering and the source citation, this writer is committing plagiarism by giving the impression that the passage is paraphrased, when it is a form of direct quotation. Words taken verbatim must be in quotation marks.

Paraphrase Without Documentation

Plagiarized: **Economic competition is at the basis of many of the world's problems. Only by seeing ourselves as a single human family without the separation of national boundaries can world tensions begin to be eased.**

Here the writer has reworded the ideas of the original into an acceptable paraphrase, but because there is no documentation (either in the text or in parentheses), the reader is led to believe that these ideas are original.

Paraphrase with Incomplete Documentation

Plagiarized (MLA): **Economic competition is at the basis of many of the world's problems (Ellis 23). Only by seeing ourselves as a single**

family without the separation of national boundaries can world tensions begin to be eased.

This paraphrase is identical to the previous one except for the addition of parenthetical documentation after the first sentence. This passage would still be considered plagiarized because the second sentence, too, is paraphrased from the original. Paraphrases of more than one sentence must be framed with documentation information that clearly marks the beginning and end of borrowed material as shown in section S-2, General Guidelines for Documenting Sources, #3.

Misrepresentation of Original Source

Misrepresented (APA): **Ellis (2013) argues that world problems are caused by overpopulation and that the only possible solution is an enforced tax on families who have more than one child (p. 23).**

The content of this passage is unrelated to the content of the original. Either as a result of careless note taking or in an attempt to make certain ideas appear more credible, writers will occasionally attribute their own ideas to other people. This practice is another form of academic dishonesty.

Acceptable (MLA): **William Ellis argues that global problems are often a result of exploitation inherent in economic competition. He contends that "grass-roots . . . people-to-people linkages irrespective of national borders" can do much to ease global tensions (23).**

This version represents one acceptable way of using the source material. The original author of the ideas is clearly identified, and words that are used verbatim are placed in quotation marks. An ellipsis is used to indicate that some of the original wording has been omitted. The lead-in at the beginning and the parenthetical page reference at the end clearly frame the borrowed material.

Citing Sources and Academic Honesty: Activities

SELF-TEST

Determine whether the information described in each case will require citation of the source. Write **Yes** or **No** on the blank line.

1. You clearly identify the source at the beginning of a paragraph that summarizes the author's ideas about teenage drinking. Because readers will naturally assume all of the ideas in the paragraph are from the source, no additional citation is necessary.   1. _____

2. In your paper on the history of aviation you state the date of the Wright brothers' first successful flight at Kitty Hawk.

2. _____

3. You create and distribute a survey at your school about the cafeteria food, and you include the results in your paper.

3. _____

4. You skim a 325-page book titled *Using the Internet*. A major theme throughout the book is that the Internet is an important technological achievement. You include this in your paper.

4. _____

5. You rephrase into your own words information that is from a government document published in the 1930s. The information is not copyrighted and is considered to be in the public domain.

5. _____

6. In a paper on the civil rights movement you find some general, well-known background information in an encyclopedia. It is obviously common knowledge, so you copy the information and include it in your paper.

6. _____

7. You talk to your mother about the steps she went through in obtaining a bank loan for a new car. You include this information in your paper.

7. _____

8. You are writing a paper on the topic of poverty in developing countries. On the Internet you find a photograph of an unidentified child and decide to use it.

8. _____

9. In your paper you decide to include the saying "A penny saved is a penny earned," which you find while scrolling through *Bartlett's Quotations* on the Internet.

9. _____

10. You find an article that takes the same position you have taken on the subject of gun control. To save time you summarize in your paper a portion of the argument from the article, since the author's ideas are identical to your own.

10. _____

11. You identify the source in parentheses at the end of a paragraph of several sentences that summarizes an author's objections to standardized testing in schools. Is any additional citation required?

11. _____

12. You find a chart from an almanac that shows the monthly ups and downs of the stock market in the year 1986. In your paper you mention only the fact that the stock remained fairly stable during this time.

12. _____

Note: To check your answers, turn to the answer key near the back of the book.

C-4 Practice in Recognizing Plagiarism

Determine whether the student version following each original excerpt is an example of correct scholarship or of plagiarism. If it is an example of plagiarism, use a separate sheet of paper to explain the reason and then write your own version without plagiarizing. Source citations and the student versions appear in MLA format, but you may give them in either MLA or APA style.

1. *Original*

As the economy weakens, black-owned firms are running up against the same problems that other small businesses face: tighter credit, rising costs and stagnant revenues. But they have other obstacles to contend with, too. Some black business people say they still have trouble borrowing from large white-run banks—a charge that bankers deny has anything to do with racial prejudice.

Mabry, Marcus. "An Endangered Dream." *Time* 3 Dec. 2013: 40–41. Print. (Quote is from page 40.)

Student Version

In addition to the usual problems all small businesses must deal with in today's shaky economy, black-owned firms may also face difficulties securing loans from white-run banks (Mabry 40).

2. Original

In the inner-city world of drugs, random violence isn't what kills children or robs them of their childhood. What kills them is their position in the drug trade: These kids, some as young as eight, have become the retailers in a business that is more dependent on child labor than any 19th century sweatshop. On the street corners, those over twenty still doing business are considered "old-timers."

Barnes, Edward. "Children of the Damned." *Life* June 2008: 30–41. Print. (Quote is from page 31.)

Student Version

Edward Barnes contends that illegal drug dealing is more dependent on child labor than any 19th century sweatshop (31).

3. Original

Alaska's wetlands provide many benefits including: food and habitat for wildlife, fish and shellfish species, natural products for human use and subsistence, shoreline erosion and sediment control, flood protection, and opportunities for recreation and esthetic appreciation.

Hall, Jonathan V., W. E. Frayer, and Bill O. Wilen. *Status of Alaska Wetlands*. 4 Nov. 1997. Web. 12 Mar. 2008.

Student Version

Alaskan wetlands offer advantages such as erosion and flood control, homes and food for wildlife, and natural beauty and products for humans' benefit.

4. Original

A new way to recycle bald tires has been developed by researchers at the University of Georgia Agricultural Experiment Station. Instead of hanging them on trees as swings, they're using them as mulch around the base.

"Tires Return as Mulch." *Popular Mechanics* 94.2 (2000): 22. LEXIS-NEXIS. Web. 31 July 2008.

Student Version

A *Popular Mechanics* article notes that University of Georgia researchers have found a new use for worn tires: instead of hanging them on trees as swings, they're using them as mulch ("Tires Return").

5. Original

It is not the divorce itself that causes children to have the problems we fear: higher rates of anxiety, depression, anger, and just being less well-adjusted. Children can develop these issues in any kind of family arrangement that is functioning in high-conflict mode. It is the conflict, the screaming or cool silence, the tension and animosity that make life miserable for children.

O'Connor, Anne. *The Truth about Stepfamilies*. New York: Marlow, 2007. Print. (Quote is from page 243.)

Student Version

What is most problematic for children of divorce is their parents' fighting, in whatever form that takes, and not the separation or divorce (243).

6. Original

It's still uncommon for the man to be the one to stay home with the kids, even if he makes less money than his wife. A lot of men say they would find it isolating to be at home; others say they would lose prestige in their careers if they took too much time off. There's still a stigma against stay-at-home dads, though this is fading some with time.

Twenge, Jean M. *Generation Me*. New York: Free Press, 2006. Print. (Quote is from page 197.)

Student Version

Stay-at-home dads still suffer from the stigma society places on them, and it's still uncommon for them to stay with their kids even if they make less money than their wives reports author of *Generation Me*, Jean Twenge. In addition, many men worry that they would lose prestige in their careers if they took too much time off (197).

7. Original

We are all worried about teenagers these days. They are shooting at each other. They are scarring their bodies with piercings and tattoos. They wear pants that sag to their crotches, tank tops that cling to their cleavage, and headphones everywhere they go. They cut class, they disrupt class, they sleep through class.

Maran, Meredith. *Class Dismissed*. New York: St. Martin's, 2007. Print. (Quote is from page 10.)

Student Version

Meredith Maran in her book *Class Dismissed* states that teens are worrying adults because of their behavior which includes violence, tattoos, and suggestive clothing (10).

8. Original

There are countless acts of humanity performed by firefighters on a daily basis. Some are small, almost trivial things that only have meaning to the people involved; others are life-altering experiences that never gain the public's attention unless there is enough drama to sell newspapers.

McCourt, Doug E. *Notes from the Firehouse*. Lynnfield, MA: McCourt Movers, 2011. Print. (Quote is from page 1.)

Student Version

McCourt asserts that firefighters help people in big and small ways every day. Such help usually is only noticed by the people it affects. Unless an event is big enough to become newsworthy, very few people will know about it even if it involves saving lives.

9. *Original*

The music of Johann Sebastian Bach (1685–1750) continues to be played throughout the world. Primarily a keyboard musician, he served as organist at Arnstadt (1703–1707), Muhlhausen (1707–1708), Weimar (1708–1717), Cothen (1717–1723), and finally Leipzig (1723–1750).

Hughes, Walden D. "J. S. Bach: Composer and Pedagogue." *Piano Quarterly* 38.3 (2008): 48–55. Print. (Quote is from page 48.)

Student Version

Johann Sebastian Bach (1685–1750) was an organist throughout his professional career, playing at Arnstadt, Muhlhausen, Weimar, Cothen, and Leipzig between 1703 and 1750.

10. *Original*

Assertive individuals tend to feel more in control of their lives, derive more satisfaction from their relationships and achieve their goals more often. They also will obtain more respect from, and inspire confidence in, those with whom they interact since they tend to be viewed as strong characters who will not be easily swayed.

Hargie, Owen, Christine Saunders, and David Dickson. *Social Skills in Interpersonal Communication.* London: Routledge, 2000. Print. (Quote is from page 271.)

Student Version

Because they are not readily influenced, assertive people gain respect from others, and they experience success in guiding their own lives, nurturing good relationships, and achieving their goals (Hargie, Saunders, and Dickson 271).

C-5 Additional Practice in Recognizing Plagiarism

Determine whether the three student versions following each original excerpt are examples of correct scholarship or of plagiarism. If they are examples of plagiarism, explain the reason on a separate sheet of paper. If all three versions are plagiarized, write your own correct version. Source citations and the student versions have been written in MLA format, but you may give them in either MLA or APA style.

1. *Original*

In the early 19th century the demand for cadavers was stimulated by advances in medical science and by the proliferation of anatomy schools. Under English law, body snatching was a misdemeanor punishable by imprisonment, but the law did not deter men from entering that profitable trade. Cemeteries became the hunting ground of body snatchers, who dug up the freshly buried dead at night and sold bodies to the highest bidder. Anxious relatives and friends often guarded the graves of the recently dead, and iron coffins as well as iron grilles for vaults were used to thwart the grave robbers.

Curtis, L. Perry Jr. "Body Snatching." *Britannica Online.* Encyclopedia Britannica, 2011. Web. 17 Jan. 2011.

Student Versions

(A) L. Perry Curtis, Jr. implies the act of body snatching increased in 19th-century England because the medical field needed more cadavers. Even though body snatching was considered a crime, men still engaged in digging up dead bodies for profit while family members tried to guard the graves of relatives who had been recently buried.

(B) Because cadavers were needed for anatomy schools in 19th-century England, physicians could be seen roaming graveyards in the middle of the night, digging up fresh corpses (Curtis).

(C) The demand for cadavers in early 19th-century England, stimulated by advances in medical science, led to an increase in the criminal act of body snatching, which took place in cemeteries, the hunting grounds for body snatchers who dug up the freshly buried dead for profit, contends L. Perry Curtis, Jr.

2. *Original*

Subway train surfaces are central to graffiti style for a number of reasons. First, graffiti murals depend on size, color, and constant movement for their visual impact. Although handball courts and other flat surfaces are suitable, they cannot replace the dynamic reception of subway facades. Unlike handball courts and building surfaces, trains pass through diverse neighborhoods, allowing communication between various black and Hispanic communities throughout the five boroughs and the larger New York population and disseminating graffiti writers' public performance.

Rose, Tricia. *Black Noise.* Hanover, London: Wesleyan Up, 2010. Print. (Quote is from page 43.)

Student Versions

(A) Because subway trains move, they play an integral role in communicating graffiti style to Black and Hispanic people in all sections of New York, claims author Tricia Rose. This transference would not be possible if the artists used surfaces

incapable of disseminating graffiti writers' public performance (43).

(B) As they pass through diverse New York neighborhoods, subway train facades provide a dynamic medium not possible with static surfaces in displaying graffiti style to Blacks and Hispanics, claims Tricia Rose, author of *Black Noise* (43).

(C) Blacks and Hispanics in New York display graffiti on marked-up subway train facades that pass through their communities. The moving nature of the trains provides them with a more dynamic medium compared to surfaces such as handball courts in their own neighborhoods, believes author Tricia Rose (43).

3. *Original*

It is really no surprise at all that there are so many small companies—often very small ones—that have come to Twitterville. Why wouldn't they? A new business located in a spare bedroom or less-than-prime former industrial space can build a network of customers all over the world at little or no cost.

Israel, Shel. *Twitterville*: *How Businesses Can Thrive in the New Global Neighborhoods*. New York: Penguin, 2009. Print.

Student Versions

(A) Only a new business or one working out of a small space, contends Shel Israel, would use a social network as trivial as Twitter to get off the ground (147.)

(B) Shel Israel, author of a book on Twitter, notes small business have experienced support from Twitter as this social medium "can build a network of customers all over the world at little or no cost" (147).

(C) Businesses that start from the ground up can increase their customer base very cheaply if they choose to use Twitter as a networking tool states Shel Israel, author of a book on Twitter (147).

4. *Original*

Analyses of eighth-grade teaching and curriculum show our country has a fragmented curriculum and teaching generally is not focused on challenging content nor is it executed in a way that promotes problem-solving skills. The majority of our students do not take advanced math or science courses, do not have a solid foundation coming out of middle school, and are not being taught by teachers fully prepared to teach math and science. As a result, by the 12th grade, U.S. ranking fell to below average in both science and mathematics, even among our advanced students.

Larson, Karen. Business Coalition for Education Reform. *The Formula for Success: A Business Leader's Guide to Supporting Math and Science Achievement*. Washington: GPO, 2011. Print. (Quote is from page 4.)

Student Versions

(A) Karen Larson, a writer for the Business Coalition for Educational Reform, claims that math and science scores for twelfth graders fell below average because most middle-school teachers of those subjects are not taking the time to prepare the material appropriately and students are too lazy to take advanced courses (4).

(B) Because eighth-grade teachers do not present math and science curriculum in ways that foster critical thinking, students test below average in these subjects internationally by the time they reach twelfth grade (4). Another factor in this equation is that a small number of students take advanced courses in math and science.

(C) Karen Larson contends that studies of eighth-grade teaching methods for math and science show that teaching is generally not focused on challenging content nor is it executed in a way that promotes problem-solving skills. Because of this and the fact that a small number of students take advanced courses in these subjects, students test below average internationally by the time they are seniors in high school (4).

5. *Original*

The sounds of instruments in Africa are considered humanlike: They are referred to as voices. These sounds are seen as an extension of the musician and not as a separate tool or object.

Ayazi-Hashjin, Sherry. *Rap and Hip Hop: The Voice of a Generation*. New York: Rosen, 1999. Print. (Quote is from page 14.)

Student Versions

(A) In Africa the sounds of musical instruments are not separated from the musician, and the sound is viewed as part of the musician's voice .

(B) Sherry Ayazi-Hashjin explains that musical instruments in Africa are not seen as the makers of the sound. These sounds are seen as an extension of the musician and not as a separate tool or object.

(C) Musicians in Africa are seen as the makers of sound, not the instruments. The sounds that come from the instruments are considered representations of human voices emphasizes author Sherry Ayazi-Hashjin (14).

S-1 When to Summarize

One of the most important skills that you will need to develop in order to incorporate secondary sources into your writing and to avoid plagiarism is *summarizing*. The ability to summarize—to restate concisely the main facts or ideas of a longer work—is useful for all kinds of learning, and it is essential for writing papers requiring secondary sources. You can summarize entire books, whole articles or essays, or just portions of your sources. Television guides often describe full-length movies and other programs, for example, with summaries of one or two sentences. Essentially, when you summarize, you state the major concepts in your own vocabulary and sentence style, omitting much of the detail of the original. Also, when you summarize a source in your paper, you do so in order to support a point you want to make. *All* source material must be directed toward the development or explanation of your own ideas. Otherwise, you run the risk of letting someone else's ideas stand for or overshadow your own.

An important reason for summarizing (and paraphrasing) is to convert passages that are difficult, jargon-ridden, or technical into language that is clearly understandable to your reader. If the meaning of a passage is difficult to determine, use the following steps to arrive at an accurate summary:

1. Look up unfamiliar words in a dictionary and substitute easy-to-understand synonyms or definitions. Then read the passage again to be sure that you understand it.
2. Change the sentence structure. After you have reread the passage, put it away so that you cannot refer to it and immediately write your own version. You should understand the passage sufficiently well to reproduce the meaning in your own sentence style and vocabulary.
3. Finally, check your summary against the original to be sure that you did not distort the meaning and that you recorded the facts accurately and spelled the names correctly.

ESSENTIAL ELEMENTS OF A GOOD SUMMARY

A good summary meets both of these criteria:

1. It accurately reflects the meaning and intention of the original without distorting or slanting the information.
2. It is completely reworded to reflect your own vocabulary and writing style.

The following excerpt is from a book by Kate Muir titled *Arms and the Woman*. Specific examples of weak summaries follow the excerpt.

> *Original:* **It would make more sense if the military took advantage of perceived, and actual, differences between men and women. When soldiers complain about the problems of integration and the resentment on both sides, these are management and leadership problems, and not the fault of women. An army which accommodates women and uses them to best advantage rather than wasting time making excuses will find integration far less painful.**

> *Weak summary (inaccurate):* **Women in the military continue to cause problems for leaders and enlisted soldiers, resulting in painful integration (Muir 196).**

This summary is inaccurate because although Muir states that integrating women into the military is still causing resentment and problems, she specifically claims that women are not the cause.

> *Weak summary (slanted):* **Because of leadership and management problems, sexual discrimination in the military is still commonplace, and few women achieve the leadership roles they deserve (Muir 196).**

The writer of this summary has given the original passage a slant by identifying sexual discrimination as the cause, something the author does not explicitly state or intend. Although it is perfectly acceptable to draw conclusions based on source information, such conclusions must be identified as your own and not confused with the summaries of those sources.

> *Weak summary (plagiarized):* **When soldiers complain about the problems of integration and the resentment on both sides, the leaders and managers should view it as an issue worth addressing (Muir 196).**

The writer has plagiarized by using some of the exact wording of the original.

> *Acceptable summary:* **The solution to integrating women into the military can be resolved by proper leadership and management, taking advantage of gender differences rather than making excuses (Muir 196).**

S-2 Documenting Summaries

The first step in summarizing source material is writing the summary accurately, without bias, in your own words and writing style—as you are asked to do in the activity in S-3.

The next step is making sure that you give credit to the author for the ideas you have summarized. MLA style requires two pieces of information for proper documentation, the author's last name and the page numbers of the material being used:

(Davidson 12–14)

APA style requires one additional piece of information, year of publication:

(Davidson, 2013, pp. 12–14)

(Notice that the APA uses the abbreviations *p.* and *pp.* for *page* and *pages* and requires commas between the elements.)

From the author's last name, your readers can easily find the complete listing for the source by referring to your Works Cited or References list, which will be arranged alphabetically according to the authors' last names. Remember that your reference list entries do not give the page numbers of specific passages. Book entries contain no page numbers at all, and article entries contain the page numbers of the *entire* article. The only way your readers will know where to find the specific passage you are documenting is by the page (or pages) you list for it *in the text.*

Page numbers can be omitted if you are citing the entire work. Page numbers are also unnecessary if you are citing one-page articles and nonprint sources without page or paragraph numbers. For example, the four-page article "NASA Fears Long Silence End of Mars Pathfinder," written by Samuel Barber and retrieved from <www.washingtonpost.com> does not include page or paragraph numbers. Cite only the author for MLA (Barber) and the author and date for APA (Barber, 2011). If the summary is longer than one sentence, create a frame and credit the source at the end in place of a page number. (See guidelines 3 and 7 that follow.)

There are three basic stylistic options for incorporating documentation, and you should be able to use them all in your writing:

Option 1. You can work all of the information about your source smoothly into the wording of your sentence. Such explanatory material is called a *lead-in.* Including a page number in the narrative or lead-in is usually a bit awkward, and placing it in parentheses is preferable. You may want to use this option when a specific page reference is unnecessary, such as with electronic sources or one-page articles.

> *MLA or APA:* **As early as page one of his 2013 book *Environmental Crises,* Martin Mahler begins uncovering the political motivation behind much of our nation's pollution problems.**

Option 2. You can put part of the source information in the narrative of your paper (or lead-in) and part of it in parentheses:

> *MLA:* **Martin Mahler argues convincingly that political interests are delaying solutions to environmental problems (1).**

> *APA:* **Mahler (2013, p. 1) argues convincingly that political interests are delaying solutions to environmental problems.**

> *or*

> **Mahler (2013) argues convincingly that political interests are delaying solutions to environmental problems (p. 1).**

Option 3. You can put all of your documentation in parentheses, usually at the end of the sentence. This method is generally used once you have established the identity of the source and now want to emphasize the ideas without repeatedly cluttering the narrative with reference information:

> *MLA:* **The cleaning of our nation's environment is often impeded by political interests (Mahler 1).**

> *APA:* **The cleaning of our nation's environment is often impeded by political interests (Mahler, 2013, p. 1).**

NOTE: The numerical systems of the *Chicago Manual of Style* and the Council of Science Editors need no rules on how to form text citations because they simply use a number (usually superscript) that corresponds to a citation at the bottom of the page (footnote) or at the end of the paper (endnote):

Political interests impede conservation efforts.[2]

It is still necessary, however, to integrate source material and mark boundaries with narrative lead-ins and signal phrases. (See point 3 in General Guidelines for Documenting Sources.)

2. Martin Mahler, *Environmental Crises* (New York: Macmillan, 2013) 1.

GENERAL GUIDELINES FOR DOCUMENTING SOURCES

1. **Lead-Ins** The first time you cite a source, it is best to use a narrative lead-in giving the author's name (first and last for MLA; last name only is acceptable for APA) and as much additional information as you can fit smoothly into your sentence. By including information about the author's background, current title or position, and level of expertise, you are doing your readers a service. The more information you provide, the more convincing and credible your source will seem:

   MLA: **Martin Mahler, a well-known advocate of environmental protection and author of several books,** states that political interests are impeding environmental cleanup (1).

   APA: **Mahler (2013), a well-known advocate of environmental protection and author of several books,** states that political interests are impeding environmental cleanup (p. 1).

   Once the identity of your source has been established, you need only mention the last name for either MLA or APA in later references.

2. **Multiple Authors** If your source has more than one author, mention the author names in the same order in which they are listed in the source:

   MLA: **Herman, Brown, and Martel predict dramatic changes in the earth's climate in the next 200 years (174).**

   APA: **Herman, Brown, and Martel (2013) predict dramatic changes in the earth's climate in the next 200 years (p. 174).**

   For later references to sources with more than three authors, both MLA and APA cite only the first author followed by the Latin abbreviation *et al.* ("and others").

   (Herman et al.)

3. **Frames** If you use a direct quote, quotation marks are used to mark the *beginning* and *end* of the source material. Summaries and paraphrases present a unique problem because no quotation marks are used. If your summary or paraphrase is longer than one sentence, it is not necessary to document each sentence, but you must make it clear that *all* of the information is from a source. You need to mark the boundaries so readers know exactly where source material begins and ends. The best way to handle this situation is to "frame" your summary with documentation information at the

beginning and end of the source material. Without the use of quotation marks, this must be done with narrative wording or parenthetical citation: *A single citation either at the beginning or end of a paragraph is insufficient.* Usually a page number in parentheses will serve as the end boundary or frame. However, if you are working with source material without page numbers (Internet sites) you will need to create a narrative lead-in for the beginning and a narrative tag at the end of multiple-sentence summaries or paraphrases. The following examples show unacceptable and acceptable methods of documenting a summary of more than one sentence. Although the formatting follows MLA style, the same general principles apply to APA.

Unacceptable: **David Hernandez, the new chair of the Federal Trade Commission, reports that consumer protection agencies seldom respond to an individual complaint (112). Instead they watch for patterns in consumer complaints (Hernandez 112). Identifying businesses that systematically violate trade regulations is an ongoing process (Hernandez 112).**

The documentation after each sentence is unnecessary and awkwardly interrupts the flow of the summary.

Unacceptable: **David Hernandez, the new chair of the Federal Trade Commission, reports that consumer protection agencies seldom respond to an individual complaint (112). Instead they watch for patterns in consumer complaints. Identifying businesses that systematically violate trade regulations is an ongoing process.**

Because the last two sentences are not documented, the reader would incorrectly assume that they are not part of the Hernandez report but are original ideas from the writer.

Unacceptable: **Consumer protection agencies seldom respond to an individual complaint. Instead they watch for patterns in consumer complaints. Identifying businesses that systematically violate trade regulations is an ongoing process (Hernandez 112).**

Because the first two sentences are not documented, the reader would incorrectly assume that they are not part of the Hernandez report but are original ideas of the writer.

Acceptable: **David Hernandez, the new chair of the Federal Trade Commission, reports that consumer protection agencies seldom respond to an individual complaint. Instead they watch** for patterns in consumer complaints. Identifying businesses that systematically violate trade regulations is an ongoing process (112).

Here the summarized material is framed with source information at the beginning (author's name in a lead-in) and at the end (page number in parentheses).

Acceptable: **Margaret Gibbs, a cardiologist at the University of California, warns that heart attacks occur when arteries become clogged with fatty deposits. Over time the deposits can become large enough to restrict blood flow. Gibbs suggests exercise and a vegetarian diet as a way to reduce the risk of heart disease.**

Here the summarized material does not have a page reference, so it is framed with source information at the beginning and a source credit in the last sentence ("Gibbs suggests . . ."). This method of framing summaries and paraphrases is necessary with Internet sources and one-page articles.

Note: With the number systems of CSE and CMS styles, a number (either in superscript or parentheses) will mark the end of a source; however it is still necessary to mark the beginning of multiple-sentence summaries with a narrative lead-in.

Acceptable: **Margaret Gibbs, a cardiologist at the University of California, warns that . . . . exercise and a vegetarian diet will reduce the risk of heart disease.[2]**

4. **No Author** If the source does not list an author, you must mention the title, since that is how it will be listed in your reference list. If you are putting that information in parentheses, you need not use the entire title, just enough so that the reader can find it.

Full Title in Lead-In

MLA: **The article "Rising Toll of Teenage Alcoholism" points out that television beer commercials present drinking role models that most young people see as desirable (17).**

APA: **The article "Rising Toll of Teenage Alcoholism" (2013) points out . . . as desirable (p. 17).**

Shortened Title in Parentheses

MLA: **A recent *New York Times* article makes the point that television beer commercials present drinking role models that most young people see as desirable ("Rising Toll" 17).**

APA: **A recent *New York Times* article makes . . . as desirable ("Rising Toll," 2013, p. 17).**

5. **More than One Source by the Same Author** If your reference list contains more than one source by the same author, you must indicate which work you are documenting by including the title (for MLA only):

MLA: **It is now theoretically possible to recreate an identical creature from any animal or plant by using the DNA contained in the nucleus of any somatic cell (Thomas, "On Cloning" 73).**

APA format includes the date of each source in all documentation, and because different works by the same author will rarely have the same date, they can be easily identified on the reference list. If two or more works by the same author *do* have the same publication date, list them alphabetically by title on the reference list, and place lowercase letters after the year to identify them in the text:

APA: **. . . of any somatic cell (Thomas, 2012a, p. 73).**

6. **Abstracts** Abstracts of articles are created to assist you in determining the usefulness of those articles, not to serve as primary source material. If an abstract seems promising, try to locate the article itself. If the original source is not available and you still want to include information from an abstract of it, indicate in your lead-in that your source is an abstract:

Unacceptable: **David Linder insists that negative feelings toward others often come from irrational beliefs.**

Acceptable: **An abstract of Linder's article "Interpersonal Relationships" states that negative feelings toward others often come from irrational beliefs.**

7. **No Page Numbers** Electronic sources usually do not have fixed page numbers or section numbering (such as numbering of paragraphs) even if the print counterpart does. Without page references, you must take care to frame summaries of more than one sentence (see guideline 3). If your electronic source has page or paragraph numbering, include it in the Works Cited or References citation and in the parenthetical citation.

Note: Do not use paragraph numbering unless the article has numbered the paragraphs.

(Hargrave, pars. 9–10).

Hargrave, Thomas. "Reflections in Literary Criticism." *Exemplaria* 10.2 (2011): 12 pars. *ProQuest.* Web. 22 June 2011.

Often, computer databases allow you to retrieve a photocopy of a source as it originally appeared in print, in which case you can use the page numbers available there.

Summarizing: Activities

S-3 Practice in Summarizing

Follow the individual directions for each exercise, and complete the exercises on a separate sheet of paper. Because summarizing the writing of others, particularly professional or technical writing, can be a difficult task in itself, the following activity is designed to give you practice, at first, with summarizing alone. Information about the source will be included in the next activity, S-4. To minimize the tendency to follow the original wording too closely, have someone read the passages aloud to you; then, without looking at the passages, summarize *using your own wording and phrasing.*

1. Write a one-sentence summary of the following passage:

   Until just a few years ago, making a baby boy or a baby girl was pretty much a hit-or-miss affair. Not anymore. Parents who have access to the latest genetic testing techniques can now predetermine their baby's sex with great accuracy.

2. Write a one-sentence summary of the following passage:

   Children of divorce have no choice. If the parent with whom they live, usually the mother, has to or wants to work, the children must pick up some of the slack. It doesn't usually hurt them. In fact, many adults of divorce, in retrospect, say that the arrangement worked amazingly well and propelled them on the road to competence and independence as an adult.

3. Write a one-sentence summary of the following passage:

   Critics on both left and right have complained that America is awash in talk about rights. No political debate proceeds for very long without one side, or both, resting its argument on rights—property rights, welfare rights, women's rights, nonsmokers' rights, the right to life, abortion rights, gay rights, gun rights, you name it.

4. Write a two-sentence summary of the following passage:

   We should not hide the fact that Columbus and other European explorers were often brutal. But there was also brutality in indigenous cultures—as well as much to be admired. And there was much to praise about Europeans as well, who did, after all, bring with them the foundations for our legal, educational, and political institutions. But instead of being encouraged to search for complicated

truth, students are increasingly presented with oversimple versions of the American past that focus on the negative.

5. Write a three-sentence summary of the following passage:

   Rhythm and blues is a form of black popular music dating from the 1940s and extending into the late 1960s and 1970s when it became known as "soul music." It is the main force linking black popular music with rock 'n' roll, rock, and other popular styles. R & B, as it is also called, is derived from earlier forms, especially the blues, the dominant mode of vocal and instrumental music among rural blacks during the early years of the 20th century. Another prime influence was black gospel music, which helped shape the style of performance and contributed to the tendency toward group singing, which persists. Emphasis on pronounced rhythms suitable for dancing is reflected in its name.

6. Write a two-sentence summary of the following passage:

   The key element in any attempt at humor is conflict. Our brain is suddenly jolted into trying to accept something that is unacceptable. The punch line of a joke is the part that conflicts with the first part, thereby surprising us and throwing our synapses into some kind of fire drill.

7. Write a three-sentence summary of the following passage:

   Out-of-wedlock births are becoming more common around the globe. In Europe, the proportion of babies born out of wedlock has doubled and tripled in the past twenty years. Many people assume that this is because European welfare states support single mothers (and the poor overall) more generously than the U.S. government does. And this belief is prevalent in a more extreme form: Some people believe that unwed mothers (especially teens) get pregnant and have a baby just to get a welfare check, and that consequently it's not surprising that European countries have increasing rates. But all industrialized countries, including the United States, are cutting back on welfare provision as a result of the tightening global economy, and out-of-wedlock births have responded by *increasing.*

8. Write a two-sentence summary of the following passage:

   The use of scorpion venom to fight glioma, a form of brain cancer, complements other scientific research in recent years on how animal poisons can be useful in treating human diseases. For example, a protein found in snake venom that causes victims to bleed to death can, in small doses, stop blood from clotting and could be an effective treatment for heart disease and stroke.

9. Write a two-sentence summary of the following passage:

When pain control is done correctly, it almost never has the side effect of hastening the patient's death. There are board-certified pain-control specialists who know how to properly set dosage and increase it if necessary as the pain worsens. People do not become addicted or permanently doped up under those circumstances.

10. Write a one-sentence summary of the following passage:

Mercy killing is defended by proponents as death with dignity when, in fact, it is an act that unfairly exploits fear of pain, suffering, indignity, abandonment, and loss of control.

S-4 Practice in Documenting Summaries

For each of the following exercises, use your summary sentences from section S-3 and include appropriate documentation as indicated, in either MLA or APA style. When creating lead-ins, use present tense verbs such as *claims, reports, notes, states.*

1. Put all necessary information for documentation in parentheses.

Lemonick, Michael D. "Designer Babies." *Time* 11 Jan. 2013: 64–65. *EBSCOhost.* Web. 27 Feb. 2008. (Text retrieved from this electronic database was a photocopy of article as it was originally printed. **Excerpt is from page 64.** See section S-2, guideline 7.)

Example

MLA: **The truly humorous American writer reveals the stupidity and silliness of human behavior (Schmitz 3).**

APA: **. . . silliness of human behavior (Schmitz, 2013, p. 3).**

2. Put all information for documentation in the narrative of the text (or lead-in).

Beal, Edward W., and Gloria Hochman. "Adult Children of Divorce." *Parenting.* Nov. 2008: 23–37. *ABI-INFORM.* Web. 22 Mar. 2009. (Text retrieved from this electronic database **does not have page numbers** even though the original article is paginated. See section S-2, guideline 7.)

Example

MLA: **In their article "Uranus," Gibbons and Amos state that for more than four billion years temperatures on the surface of Uranus have not risen above minus 346°F.**

APA: **In their 2013 article "Uranus," Gibbons and Amos state. . . .**

3. Put information for documentation partly in the narrative of the text (or lead-in) and partly in parentheses **using paragraph reference instead of page reference** for this electronic source. (See section S-2, guideline 7.) In your research, you have discovered that David Boaz is a professor of political science. Assume that this is the first time you are using this source, and you want to include this information in your lead-in to clarify for your readers who this person is and why his ideas are important.

Boaz, David. *Libertarianism.* June 2008. 16 pars. *Google Scholar.* Web. 12 May 2009. (Excerpt is from paragraph 6.)

Example

MLA: **In *Of Huck and Alice,* Neil Schmitz, author of several books about American humor, states that the truly humorous writer deals with life's tragedies (par. 10).**

APA: **In *Of Huck and Alice,* Schmitz (2009), author of several books about American humor, states . . . tragedies (par. 10).**

4. Put information for documentation partly in the narrative of the text (or lead-in) and partly in parentheses, because that is the best way to handle a summary of more than one sentence.

Cheney, Lynne V. *Telling the Truth.* New York: Simon, 2005. Print. (**Excerpt is from page 94.**)

Example

MLA: **Schaller, Blair, and Phelps claim that the first live panda to reach the United States arrived in 1936. It was eventually acquired by the Chicago Zoo (286).**

APA: **Schaller, Blair, and Phelps (2011) claim . . . Chicago Zoo (p. 286).**

5. Frame this summary with source information at the beginning and end. (See section S-2, guideline 3.) [*Hint:* Since this encyclopedia entry lists no author, you must document the source by its title. Also, page numbers are unavailable with this online source, so the second citation is required to indicate where your summary ends. Note that in the following example the second internal documentation ("According to the Encyclopaedia Britannica . . .") makes it clear that the entire passage is from a source by providing a frame at the end.]

"Rhythm and Blues." *Encyclopaedia Americana Online.* Encyclopaedia Americana Foundation, 2007. Web. 12 July 2011.

Example

MLA: **The encyclopedia entry "Newton, Sir Isaac" points out that the scientific revolution in England reached its high point with Newton's theory of gravity. He was a member of the Royal Society, founded in 1622. According to** *Encyclopaedia Britannica Online,* **the primary purpose of this organization was to serve as a forum for scientific discussions on theories such as Newton's.**

APA: **The encyclopedia entry "Newton, Sir Isaac" (2011) points out that. . . . According to the** *Encyclopaedia Britannica Online* **. . . such as Newton's.**

6. Put information for documentation partly in the narrative and partly in parentheses. Assume that this is the first time you are using this source. In your research, you have discovered that Gary Larson is an internationally acclaimed cartoonist and the author of *Far Side* cartoons.

Larson, Gary. *The PreHistory of the Far Side.* Kansas City, MO: Andrews, 2007. Print. **(Excerpt is from page 160.)**

Example

MLA: **Cliff Tarpy, author of** *San Francisco Bay* **and TV weatherman, explains how the warm coastal waters moderate the climate and cause the well-known San Francisco fog. In the summer warm inland air rises, drawing the fog in. In the winter warm ocean air rises, drawing the fog out (23).**

APA: **Tarpy (2011), author of** *San Francisco Bay.* **. . . drawing the fog out (p. 23).**

7. Put the information for documentation in the narrative of the text (or lead-in). The lead-in should also identify the source as an abstract since abstracts are not from the original text and are often written by someone other than the author. (See section S-2, guideline 6.) Since the abstract itself does not have page numbers, an end frame must be created using a source credit in the last sentence. (See section S-2, guideline 3.)

Luker, Kristin. "The Politics of Teenage Pregnancy." *Teen Parents* 2.3 (2008): 6–7. Abstract. *Ebscohost.* Web. 27 Aug. 2011.

Example

MLA: **The abstract of Parker's article "Acid Rain: Rhetoric and Reality" provides several examples of the complexity of the problem of acid rain and the wide spectrum of issues involved. For example, the abstract discusses the complex international implications of acid rain.**

APA: **The abstract of Parker's (2009) article. . . . For example, the abstract discusses . . . implications of acid rain.**

8. Put information for documentation at the beginning and end of your summary to create a frame for this electronic source without page numbers. Use the article title, since no author is listed. (See section S-2, guideline 3.)

"Scorpion Venom May Hold Brain Cancer Cure." *National Geographic Online.* National Geographic. 10 Mar. 2008. Web. 15 Mar. 2009.

Example

MLA: **The article "From Cinderella to Harry Potter" presents the complexities of children's stories. The article documents how fantasy stories are often based upon real-life experiences of the author.**

APA: **"From Cinderella to Harry Potter" (2011) states that. . . . The article documents . . . of the author.**

9. Put information for documentation partly in the narrative and partly in parentheses. Assume that this is the first time you are using this source in your paper and that you are using two sources written by this author. (The second source is in the following exercise.) In your research, you have discovered that Wesley Smith is a nationally recognized lawyer who argues against assisted suicide. (*Hint:* In MLA format, it is necessary to mention both author and title to differentiate sources written by the same person.)

Smith, Wesley. "In the Name of Compassion." Interview. By Mark O'Brien. *The Sun* Feb. 2008: 9–14. Print. **(Excerpt is from page 11.)**

Example

MLA: **James D. Darling, a zoologist who has been studying whales for over two decades, concludes that whales are closely related to mammals such as bison, pigs, and cattle. Their mating system and social behavior are very similar ("Whales" 885).**

APA: **Darling (2012), a zoologist who has . . . are very similar (p. 885).**

In APA format, dates will usually identify different works by the same author. If dates happen to be the same, arrange the works alphabetically by title in the references list and place lowercase letters after the year (for example, 2007a and 2007b).

10. Put information for documentation partly in the text and partly in parentheses. Assume that you are using more than one source written by this author in your paper. (See Exercise 9 above for a sample, except one-page articles like this one do not require page citation.)

Smith, Wesley. "Don't Turn Docs into Killers." *USA Today* 25 Oct. 2007: 12A. Print.

S-5 Practice in Writing and Documenting Summaries

Write the indicated number of summary sentences for each passage. Document the sentences according to MLA or APA format as instructed. When creating lead-ins, use present tense verbs such as *claims, reports, notes, states.*

1. For MLA style, put all information for documentation in the narrative of the text (or lead-in), because no page numbers are available for this electronic source. Summary length: one sentence.

   For APA style, put all information for documentation in parentheses. (*Hint:* Since the encyclopedia entry lists no author, you must cite the source by article title.)

   Certain commonly performed cosmetic procedures are potentially dangerous. For example, too frequent or harsh brushing of the hair may cause scalp irritation. Tight curling of the hair may cause temporary or even permanent hair loss, and pushing back the nail cuticle may provide an opening for infection. Bathing or showering too often during dry weather can result in removing the natural oils from the skin surface and thus lead to "winter itch" and eczema.

   "Skin." *Encyclopedia Americana Online.* Encyclopedia Americana. 2007. Web. 19 July 2011.

2. Put all information for documentation in the narrative of the text (or lead-in), because no page numbers are available for this electronic source. Summary length: one sentence.

   Levis are fading, and khakis are to blame. Levi Strauss announced last week that it will stop making blue jeans for 60 days at seven U.S. plants to burn off a mountain of unsold pants. The wave had been building for years because denim pants are losing their fashion edge. Stonewashed, wide flares, or relaxed fit, Levis are no longer the second skin for American customers.

McConnell, Doug. "A Levi Lament." *San Francisco Chronicle Online.* San Francisco Chronicle, 9 Nov. 2008. Web. 9 Feb. 2011.

3. Put information for documentation partly in the text (or lead-in) and partly in parentheses. Assume that this is the first time you have cited this source. In your research, you have discovered that Ron Howard teaches in the Harvard MBA program. Summary length: two sentences.

   The unique ability to juggle multiple thoughts at the same time is called multitasking. Through multitasking, humans can rapidly shift their attention back and forth from one task or thought to another, which allows them, for example, to talk on the phone while watching television. The impression this creates is that people are doing both simultaneously. In reality, they attend to one for a bit, switch attention to the other, and then switch back again. If they are focusing on the television show and the person on the phone says something particularly startling, their attention will be drawn back to the conversation.

   Howard, Ron. *TechnoStress.* New York: Wiley, 2008. Print. (Excerpt is from page 107.)

4. Put information for documentation partly in the text (or lead-in) at the beginning and at the end of your summary to create a frame for this electronic source without page numbers. (See section S-2, guideline 3.) Summary length: three sentences.

   An increasing number of college students desire to participate in activities outside the classroom, including volunteer activities in the local communities. Most students are confronted with time constraints that force them to limit their involvement to a select number of activities. This is especially true for students who need to work in order to pay for a portion of their education expenses. For many of them, the combination of classes, study time, and one or more part-time jobs severely limits their ability to participate in volunteer activities. Federal Work Study community service jobs provide these students with the option of combining the financial need to work with the personal goal of helping the local community.

   United States. U.S. Department of Education. *Expanding Federal Work-Study and Community Service Opportunities.* 2007. Web. 14 Oct. 2011.

5. Put information for documentation partly in the text (or lead-in) and partly in parentheses. Summary length: one sentence.

   It is all too easy to dismiss other people's religious beliefs as superstition; yet a belief system can prove helpful and, in an age of hitherto unbelievable technological possibilities, perhaps we need moral and ethical guidance more than ever before, and for that reason all spiritual beliefs are valuable.

Seleba, Anne. *Mother Teresa: Beyond the Image.* New York: Doubleday, 2007. (Excerpt is from page 195.)

6. Put information for documentation partly in the text (or lead-in) and partly in parentheses. Assume that this is the first time you have cited this source. In your research, you have discovered that Craig Soderholm has completed a landmark study on the effects that communication habits have had on the success of CEOs in the 1990s. Summary length: one sentence.

While physiologists estimate that people are capable of over twenty thousand different facial expressions in both voluntary and involuntary muscles, most people are not satisfied with their natural appearance. Instead, they modify it with cosmetic, physical, and even surgical changes—some to appear what they consider more attractive, younger, or older, more serious or less serious, more physically fit and active; some to better express what they feel is their identity, or on the opposite side of the coin, to hide or change their identity; and some, simply for fun and variety.

Soderholm, Craig E. *How 10% of the People Get 90% of the Pie.* New York: St. Martin's, 2007. Print. (Excerpt is from page 134.)

7. Put information for documentation partly in the text (or lead-in) and partly in parentheses. Assume that this is the first time you have cited this source. In your research, you have discovered that Anne Meyer directs the Schools Without Drugs Council. Summary length: one sentence.

One of the greatest services that parents and educators can perform is to provide a consistent and clear message about drug use. Parents and educators *must,* by their comments and conduct, let students know that drug and alcohol use is wrong and harmful.

Meyer, Anne. *Schools Without Drugs: The Challenge.* Washington: GPO, 2009. Print. (Excerpt is from page 115.)

8. Put all information for documentation in parentheses. Summary length: one sentence.

There is no doubt that our attitude and mental outlook can strongly affect the degree to which we suffer when we are in physical pain. Let's say, for instance, that two individuals, a construction worker and a concert pianist, suffer the same finger injury. While the amount of physical pain might be the same for both individuals, the construction worker might suffer very little and in fact rejoice if the injury resulted in a month of paid vacation

which he or she was in need of, whereas the same injury could result in intense suffering to the pianist who viewed playing as his or her primary source of joy in life.

Cutler, Howard C., and His Holiness the Dalai Lama. *The Art of Happiness.* New York: Riverhead, 2008. Print. (Excerpt is from page 209.)

9. Put information for documentation partly in the text (or lead-in) and partly in parentheses. Assume that this is the first time you have cited this source. In your research, you have discovered that Mark Derr is an expert dog handler who has worked with the dogs of such celebrities as Jewel Kilcher, Sylvester Stallone, and Tiger Woods. Summary length: two sentences.

Generally, scent dogs are trained on substances they are seeking, but because human cadavers are difficult to obtain, narcotics are tempting to keep around, and explosives are dangerous, some trainers will try to use substitutes or pseudo scents. In training puppies, hunters have long used the pelt or wing, if not the whole carcass of the game they want their dogs to find. The Italians substitute moldy fontina cheese for mushrooms in training their hounds, an act appearing to be an olfactory oxymoron. But the use of chemicals created to resemble a real narcotic or person is somewhat more controversial, because of concerns that dogs trained on pseudo scent will not, in fact, detect the real thing, paving the way for serious court challenges or even loss of life.

Derr, Mark. *Dog's Best Friend.* New York: Holt, 2007. Print. (Excerpt is from page 115.)

10. Put all information for documentation in the text (or lead-in) because there is no page number with this online source. Assume that this is the first time you have cited this source. In your research, you have discovered that Kay McElrath Johnson is a freelance journalist in Anchorage, Alaska. She has written award-winning articles on the Iditarod. Summary length: one sentence.

In many respects Kimarie Hanson was a typical high school senior last year. She attended class and played sports. She did her homework and made plans for the future. But Kimarie didn't want to be a typical teenager. At 18 years of age, Kimarie raced through the Alaskan wilderness to become the youngest woman to ever complete the Iditarod Trail Sled Dog Race.

Johnson, Kay McElrath. "Youthful Ambitions." *Mushing On-Line.* Jan./Feb. 2009. Web. 9 Feb. 2011.

P-1 When to Paraphrase

A *paraphrase* (or *indirect quotation*, as it is also called) restates another person's ideas in your own words. Unlike a summary, it is used with short passages—usually a sentence or two—and it does not necessarily condense or shorten the original.

Paraphrasing is necessary because as you incorporate source material into your paper, you cannot simply string together a series of quotations from a variety of sources. The material must be integrated into a consistent and even style. Also, by recasting the ideas of your sources into your own words, you maintain control over the material and can more easily use it to support and develop your own views. If you have trouble restating a passage, you probably do not understand it thoroughly. Ideas that are paraphrased have been assimilated, a process far different from copying material word for word.

As with summaries, paraphrases must be accurate, undistorted, and *completely* rewritten into your own wording and sentence structure. The most blatant form of plagiarism is following too closely the wording of another writer while giving the impression that the wording is your own. To avoid plagiarism in your paraphrases (or summaries), consider the following suggestions:

1. Rearrange the order of the information in the original.
2. Have a thesaurus or dictionary handy and look up synonyms for keywords.
3. Rephrase complex material into easy-to-understand sentences.
4. If you retain unusual terminology or phrases from the original, enclose them in quotation marks.

Original: Katy Perry's song "Hot n Cold" presents her as a prophet of the heart, torching romantic sentimentality with a firestorm of unforgiving words.

Weak paraphrase: "Hot n Cold" by Katy Perry offers a grim prophecy of love by torching romantic sentimentality with a firestorm of harsh lyrics.

The words "torching romantic sentimentality" and "firestorm" should be in quotation marks, if they are used at all, because they are unique phrases of the original.

Acceptable paraphrase: One critic notes that the "firestorm of unforgiving words" in Katy Perry's "Hot n Cold" describe a difficult relationship with grim realism.

or

"Hot n Cold" by Katy Perry offers a dark vision of love with its biting lyrics that carry the listener beyond shallow emotionalism.

In the first acceptable example, the borrowed phrase is identified with quotation marks; in the second, the wording has been completely changed, although the meaning has been accurately preserved.

P-2 Documenting Paraphrases and Using Lead-Ins

Because you must acknowledge the source of all ideas that are not your own, you must provide documentation with all paraphrases. As with summaries, source information can be identified with your choice of one of three stylistic options. Documentation can be placed (1) entirely in the narrative of the text, (2) partly in the text and partly in parentheses, or (3) entirely in parentheses. (See section S-2.)

OPTIONS FOR LEAD-INS

As explained earlier, whenever you place information about the source in the narrative of your paper, you are creating a *lead-in* or *tag*. The first time you cite a source, it is preferable to give both first and last name and some information about the author. A lead-in can be placed at the beginning, as in the following paraphrase (lead-in is underlined):

MLA: James Prochaska, a professor at Harvard's medical school, states that more than 300,000 Americans die annually as a direct result of tobacco smoking (31).

APA: Prochaska (2013), a professor at Harvard's medical school, states that . . . smoking (p. 31).

A lead-in can be placed in the middle (lead-in is underlined):

MLA: Despite the fact that the U.S. public has been warned for years about the serious health threat posed by tobacco smoking, James Prochaska, a professor at Harvard's medical school, believes that more than 300,000 Americans die annually as a direct result (31).

APA: **Despite the fact . . . Prochaska (2013), a professor at Harvard's medical school, believes that . . . result . . . (p. 31).**

Or a lead-in can be placed at the end (lead-in is underlined):

> **MLA: More than 300,000 Americans die annually as a direct result of tobacco smoking, <u>asserts James Prochaska, a professor at Harvard's medical school</u> (31).**

> **APA: More than 300,000 Americans . . . smoking, <u>asserts Prochaska (2013), a professor at Harvard's medical school</u> (p. 31).**

Literary Present Tense

Even though most sources have been written in the past, it is preferable to cast all lead-ins in "literary present tense." Note that any number of active verbs can be used. Avoid repetition and be exact in your word choice. Consider the following list:

accepts	concedes	negates
acknowledges	declares	notes
adds	denies	observes
affirms	describes	outlines
agrees	disagrees	proposes
argues	discusses	refutes
asserts	disputes	rejects
believes	emphasizes	reports
cautions	endorses	responds
challenges	explains	shows
claims	grants	suggests
comments	highlights	thinks
confirms	implies	urges
contends	insists	verifies
contradicts	maintains	writes

Paraphrasing: Activities

P-3 Practice in Paraphrasing

On a separate sheet of paper, write a *one-sentence paraphrase* of each of the following sentences. Try to include most of the information from the excerpt in your sentence without using any of the original wording.

Because paraphrasing the writing of others, particularly professional or technical writing, can be difficult, the following activity is designed to give you practice, at first, with paraphrasing alone. Do not include information about the sources at this time. To minimize the chances of following the wording of the original too closely, first read the passages and then create your paraphrases *using your own wording and phrasing* without looking at the originals again.

1. If we want to do something about violence, we have to do something about education, about jobs, about TV violence, about the myriad social problems for which we have no answers.

2. In the 5 million years since we hominids separated from apes, our DNA has evolved less than 2%.

3. Not only do animals provide companionship and devotion, they also lower our blood pressure, ease our stress, and according to some researchers, even prolong our lives.

4. We tell girls that they must be big and strong if they want to succeed at certain sports such as basketball, but the minute the game is over we expect them to go back to the skinny, anorexic look.

5. Central to Hinduism is the belief in karma, the cosmic law of cause and effect, in which each person creates his or her destiny based on his or her actions.

P-4 Practice in Documenting Paraphrases

Rewrite your paraphrases from section P-3 to include appropriate lead-ins and documentation as directed. Information about the sources for each of the quotes in section P-3 follows. Assume that in each exercise you are using the source for the first time and will, therefore, want to include some information about the author; for MLA format, use first and last names. Use a variety of present-tense active verbs with your lead-ins. (See section P-2 for examples of the different placement options of lead-ins and a list of active verbs.)

1. (a) Put the lead-in in the middle of the paraphrase. In your research, you have discovered that Jennifer Allen has completed a research study on the causes of violence.

    (b) Put the lead-in at the end.

    Allen, Jennifer. "The Danger Years." *New York Times* 21 Dec. 2013, late ed.: C7–C8. *Ebscohost*. Web. 4 Jan. 2011. (The text retrieved from this electronic database does not have page numbers, even though the original article is paginated.)

2. (a) Put the lead-in at the beginning of the paraphrase, using parentheses for the page reference. In your research, you have discovered that Walter Isaacson is a senior staff writer for *Time* who specializes in science and medicine.

    (b) Put all documentation in parentheses (no lead-in).

    Isaacson, Walter. "The Biotech Century." *Time* 11 Jan. 2013: 42–43. Print. (**Excerpt is from page 43.**)

3. (a) Put the lead-in at the end of the paraphrase, using parentheses for the page reference. In your research, you have discovered that Karen Dale Dustman is a nationally recognized veterinarian.

    (b) Put the lead-in at the beginning, using parentheses for the page reference.

    Dustman, Karen Dale. "Is Your Dog a Doctor?" *Natural Healing* Jan./Feb. 2013: 62–64. Print. (**Excerpt is from page 62.**)

4. (a) Put the lead-in in the middle of your paraphrase. In your research, you have discovered that Jesse Sherwood is a former member of the United States Olympic women's basketball team.

    (b) Put the lead-in at the end.

    Sherwood, Jesse. "Conflicting Values in Women's Sports." *Miami Herald Online*. Miami Herald, 18 Apr. 2008. Web. 20 Apr. 2008. (*Hint:* No page reference available.)

5. (a) Put the lead-in at the end of the paraphrase, using parentheses for the page reference. In your research, you have discovered that Anne Cushman and Jerry Jones have traveled extensively in India.

    (b) Put the lead-in at the beginning of the paraphrase, using parentheses for the page reference.

Cushman, Anne, and Jerry Jones. *From Here to Nirvana.* New York: Riverhead, 2008. Print. (**Excerpt is from page 54.**)

P-5 Practice in Writing and Documenting Paraphrases

Write a one-sentence paraphrase for each quotation, including the lead-in and documentation as indicated. Follow the format for either MLA or APA.

1. Put the lead-in at the end of the paraphrase. (*Hint:* No page reference available.)

    The oldest and most widely accepted view of our natural environment is that it is man's personal property at our disposal to be consumed, ornamented, or destroyed as we wish.

    Levine, William. "The Long-Term Effects of Eco-Tourism." University of Wassau Department of Environmental Sciences. May 2006. Web. 21 June 2011.

2. Put all documentation in parentheses.

    Our new understanding of the interrelatedness of all life does not seem to stop us from walking bootshod over the open face of nature, subjugating and exploiting it.

    Thomas, Lewis. *Lives of a Cell.* Boston: Viking, 2012. Print. (Excerpt is from page 102.)

3. Put the lead-in at the beginning of the paraphrase, using parentheses for the page reference.

    Paleontologists have studied many of the areas humans have reached within the past 50,000 years, and in every one, human arrival coincided with massive extinctions.

    Diamond, Jared. "Playing Dice with Megadeath." *Discover* Apr. 2002: 22–27. Print. (Excerpt is from page 23.)

4. Put the lead-in in the middle of the paraphrase, using parentheses for the page reference. Assume that this is the first time you have cited this source. In your research, you have discovered that Michael Huebner is a respected professor of environmental law at University of California, Berkeley.

    A recent Gallup poll indicated that 76 percent of Americans regard themselves as "environmentalists," and yet truly crucial issues such as air and water pollution and the near extinction of thousands of plant and animal species are treated with only passing concern.

    Huebner, Michael. *The Future of Environmentalism.* New York: Scribner's, 2005. Print. (Excerpt is from page 122.)

5. Put the lead-in in the middle of the paraphrase, using parentheses for the page reference.

Increasing concentrations of greenhouse gases in the atmosphere are expected to raise the earth's average temperature from four to eight degrees Fahrenheit over the next 100 years, causing ocean levels to rise as polar icecaps melt.

Jacobson, Jodi L. "Holding Back the Sea." *The Futurist* Sept./Oct. 2000: 56–62. Print. (Excerpt is from page 56.)

6. Put the lead-in at the beginning of the paraphrase, using parentheses for the page reference. Assume that this is the first time you have cited this source. In your research, you have discovered that Paul R. Ehrlich and Anne H. Ehrlich direct a research team for the Department of Agriculture in Washington, D.C. They are studying the effects of global warming on farming in the United States.

Crop failures due to global warming alone might result in the premature deaths of a billion or more people in the next few decades.

Ehrlich, Paul R., and Anne H. Ehrlich. *The Population Explosion.* New York: Simon, 2000. Print. (Excerpt is from page 171.)

7. Put all the documentation in parentheses at the end of the paraphrase. (*Hint:* No page reference available.)

To have a healthy environment we will have to give up things we like; we may even have to give up things we have come to think of as necessities.

Stewart, John. "Meeting the Future." *Seattle Times Online.* Seattle Times, 14 Apr. 2008. Web. 3 May 2011.

8. Put the lead-in at the beginning of the paraphrase, using parentheses for the page reference. Assume that this is the first time you have cited this source. In your research, you have discovered that Paul Konstas is a renowned anthropologist who specializes in the study of overpopulation.

Our aversion to limiting the size of the human population is built into our genes and our culture and is as deep and pervasive as the roots of human sexual behavior.

Konstas, Paul. *The Thin Edge.* New York: Basic, 2004. Print. (Excerpt is from page 36.)

9. Put all documentation in parentheses. (*Hint:* No page reference available.)

One aspect of the environmental issue that receives very little coverage in the press is overpopulation, and yet there is no issue that more dramatically affects the quality of life on this planet.

"Environmental Issues Receive Uneven Attention." Editorial. *Washington Post Online* 11 Sept. 2007. Proquest. Web. 25 July 2011.

10. Put all documentation in the lead-in at the beginning of the paraphrase.

The mentality that exploits and destroys the natural environment is the same that abuses racial and economic minorities.

Berry, Wendell. "Think Little." *The Endangered Earth.* Eds. Sarah Morgan and Dennis Okerstrom. Boston: Allyn, 2012. 417–425. Print. (Excerpt is from page 418.)

P-6 Additional Practice in Writing and Documenting Paraphrases

Write a one-sentence paraphrase for each quotation, including the lead-in and documentation as indicated. Follow the format for either MLA or APA.

1. Put the lead-in at the beginning of the paraphrase, using parentheses for the page reference. Assume that you are using two works by the same author (see exercise 2 below). In your research, you have discovered that James Cappela holds a Ph.D. in sociology and has completed extensive research on gender-specific dream patterns.

Research on dreams has shown that the average person will devote the equivalent of fifty thousand hours or six full years to dreaming and that men and women have consistently different dream content.

Cappela, James. *Dream Studies.* Englewood Cliffs, NJ: Prentice Hall, 2007. Print. (Excerpt is from page 43.)

2. Put the lead-in at the end of the paraphrase. (Remember that you are using two works by the same author and paragraphs have been numbered with this Internet source. See section S-2, guideline 7.)

Men are more likely to dream in black and white, and to dream of competing and fighting, while women's dreams are generally set indoors and involve relationships.

Cappela, James. "Dream Weaver." *Discovery Online* Dec. 2012: 12 pars. Web. 20 May 2013. (Excerpt is from paragraph 7.)

3. Put all documentation in parentheses. (*Hint:* No author is listed and no page reference is available.)

Predating Freud by over 2,000 years, Aristotle wrote that sensory function is reduced in sleep, favouring the susceptibility of dreams to emotional distortions.

"Diverse Views on the Nature of Dreams." *Encyclopaedia Britannica Online*. Encyclopaedia Britannica, 2013. Web. 17 Mar. 2013.

4. Put the lead-in in the middle of the paraphrase, using parentheses for the page reference.

Freud believed that repressed desires, especially those associated with hostility and sexuality, were released during dreams because the inhibitions of wakefulness were lessened.

Cane, Kathleen. *Understanding Dreams*. New York: Appleton, 2013. Print. (Excerpt is from page 28.)

5. Put the lead-in at the beginning of the paraphrase, using parentheses for the page reference.

Psychologists have long recognized that the symbols appearing in our dreams can mean different things to different people, and yet common meanings do occur just as common threads run through our shared daily cultural experiences.

Morory, David. *Dream Lexicon*. New York: Dekker, 1998. Print. (Excerpt is from page 114.)

6. Put the lead-in in the middle of the paraphrase, using parentheses for the page reference. Assume that this is the first time you have cited this source. In your research, you have discovered that Paul Dokes is a psychiatrist who uses dream analysis in treating his patients.

Most people have slightly more negative than positive dream experiences and often will spend weeks hammering away at a single theme, even though imagery and characters may change.

Dokes, Paul. *Clinical Uses of Dreams*. London: Hogarth, 2012. Print. (Excerpt is from page 54.)

7. Put the lead-in at the end of the paraphrase, using parentheses for the page reference.

In the highly developed civilizations of ancient Greece, Egypt, and Babylonia, diviners or seers responsible for dream interpretation often had great political and social influence.

Kramer, Margaret. *The Universality of Typical Dreams*. Chicago: Lippincott, 1995. Print. (Excerpt is from page 84.)

8. Put the lead-in in the middle of the paraphrase, using parentheses for the page reference.

In the Bible the account of Pharaoh's dream of seven fat and seven lean cows came to represent the foretelling of years of famine following years of plenty.

Zuiderhoff, Mary. "Dreams as a Source of Divination." *Psychology Today* 14 Sept. 2010: 53–54+. Print. (Excerpt is from page 54.)

9. Put all documentation in parentheses.

In Classical Greece, ailing people would come to oracular temples in order to have dreams that could be used by the priests and priestesses in prescribing cures for their sicknesses.

Lora, George. "The Demography of Dreams." *International Journal of Social Psychiatry* 24.2 (2007): 46–51. *Google Scholar*. 7 Aug. 2013. (The text retrieved from this Internet source does not have page numbers even though the original article is paginated. See section S-2, guideline 7.)

10. Put the lead-in at the beginning of the paraphrase, using parentheses for the page reference. Assume that this is the first time you have cited this source. In your research, you have discovered that Chester Maury is a professor of British literature and has written several articles and a book on dream symbolism in eighteenth-century British poetry.

The English poet Samuel Taylor Coleridge stated that he fell asleep while reading about a Mongol conqueror, and when he woke he wrote down the fully developed poem, "Kubla Khan," apparently a product of creative dreaming.

Maury, Chester. *Dream Symbolism*. Evanston, IL: McDougal, 2013. Print. (Excerpt is from page 21.)

Q-1 When to Use Direct Quotations

Direct quotations are used when you want to preserve the original wording of your source; therefore, there should be something noteworthy about all direct quotations. If you can convey the idea just as effectively in your own words in a summary or a paraphrase, you should do so. You should be the speaker in the majority of your paper, which means that you should express your own ideas and support those ideas with source information that has been thoroughly assimilated and recast into your own style. Unless the language of the source is relevant as in the explication of literary works, *no more than about 15 percent of your paper should be directly quoted material.* Readers usually pass over sections of writing that contain large amounts of quoted material. Readers want to know *your* ideas on a subject and are not impressed by long quotations taken from other writers. Reserve your use of direct quotations for dramatic phrases and especially appropriate discussions. Direct quotations are best saved for the following situations:

1. To preserve especially vivid, well-phrased, or dramatic statements.

2. To preserve the wording of someone who is well known.

3. To preserve the accuracy of a statement that might be easily misinterpreted in a paraphrase or a summary.

Q-2 Documenting and Integrating Direct Quotations

One of the most important differences between direct quotations and paraphrases or summaries involves the use of narrative lead-ins. *All direct quotations must have lead-ins; they usually also require a sentence or two following to explain their significance.* As noted earlier, paraphrases and summaries may be documented by citing all source information in parentheses rather than in a narrative lead-in, as the following paraphrase in MLA format illustrates:

> **Indonesia is the tenth largest fish-producing nation in the world (Bailey 25).**

Such an option is *not acceptable* with direct quotations. Because they use the exact words of another person,

direct quotations must be integrated into your discussion with some kind of narrative lead-in. It is also a good practice to explain the importance of the quotation in your discussion rather than expecting the reader to see the connection. Sometimes beginning writers will simply "float" a direct quotation in a paragraph without introducing it with a narrative lead-in or explaining its significance, as in the following excerpt written in MLA format:

> *"Floating"* quotation: **From Ayurvedic medicine to aromatherapy, Western medicine is beginning to take heed of nontraditional approaches to better health and well-being. "Certain aromas increase alpha waves in the back of the head associated with a more relaxed state" (Hirsch 60). Massage therapy and acupuncture are also noted for their ability to induce relaxation and relieve tension associated with disorders such as migraine headaches.**

Even though the direct quotation is correctly documented and punctuated, the writer has not integrated it with a lead-in, an explanation, or a commentary on the quotation's purpose. Here is the writer's revision of that paragraph, with the narrative lead-in and commentary sentence underlined:

> *Integrated* quotation: **From Ayurvedic medicine to aromatherapy, Western medicine is beginning to take heed of nontraditional approaches to better health and well-being. <u>Alan Hirsch, M.D., the director of neurology at the Smell and Taste Treatment and Research Foundation in Chicago, reports,</u> "Certain aromas increase alpha waves in the back of the head associated with a more relaxed state" (60). <u>Just as music can affect our emotions, studies show that smells, too, apparently produce different psychological states and can improve health as a result.</u> Massage therapy and acupuncture are also noted for their ability to induce relaxation and release tension associated with disorders such as migraine headaches.**

LEAD-INS

As with summaries and paraphrases, direct quotations can have lead-ins or tags placed at the beginning, middle, or end of the sentence, and the amount of information that is put in parentheses will depend on what information is given in the lead-in. Notice that commas are used to set off the lead-ins from the quoted material, and the first word of a quoted sentence is always capitalized.

Lead-In at the Beginning with Explanatory Sentence

MLA: A recent *Chicago Tribune* editorial asserts, "America has no trade policy, only an anti-trade policy of rules and regulations limiting U.S. sales abroad" (Eason 14). Although slightly overstated, such a position does suggest the direction policymakers have been taking.

APA: . . . U.S. sales abroad" (Eason, 2013, p. 14). Although slightly. . . .

Lead-In in the Middle with Explanatory Sentence

MLA: "There is a widespread belief among the American public," notes Isador Gorn, "that one can acquire an education, like a suntan, by mere exposure" (43). His views are shared by many people who think that too much responsibility is placed on the teacher's performance rather than the student's.

APA: . . . the American public," notes Isador Gorn (2013), "that one can acquire an education, like a suntan, by mere exposure" (p. 43). . . .

Lead-in at the End with Explanatory Sentence

MLA: America is going solar, but not in the way many people have dreamed about," claims Roger Pollak (32). He explains that it is not as simple and inexpensive as many people had supposed.

APA: . . . people have dreamed about," claims Roger Pollak (2013, p. 32). He explains. . . .

Q-3 Rules for Punctuating Quotations

1. Direct quotations require narrative lead-ins, which are set off from the quotation with commas. Narrative lead-ins or tags may be placed at the beginning, in the middle, or at the end of a direct quotation. (See sections Q-2 Documenting Direct Quoatations and Q-6 Practice in Creating Lead-ins for examples of different placement.)

   William Barnes claims, "The causes of apartheid are rooted in historical practices of economic exploitations."
   Note: Always capitalize the first word of a quoted sentence.

2. Quotations of more than four lines (MLA) or more than forty words (APA) are set off in "block format." Indent ten spaces (five spaces for APA) and

omit the quotation marks. A colon is generally used with *a full-sentence lead-in* to introduce long quotations.

Sample from Student Essay (MLA)

Grout tells us that in 1580 a group of cultivated men in Florence met at the home of Count Giovanni Bardi to revive the fine arts of ancient Greece:

> They became fired with the ambition to revive classical Greek drama, with the choruses and choral dances that accompanied the old tragedies. Aristotle had defined tragedy as "an imitation of some action . . . with language rendered pleasurable by means of rhythm, melody, and meter." From an attempt to re-create tragedy, opera was born.
>
> While serious opera was developing, the fun-loving Neapolitans began to write short, comic scenes to music. (460)

With long quotations set off in block format, retain double quotation marks for internal quotations. Also, indicate the paragraph breaks in the original source by indenting an additional three spaces, as in the sample. If you are quoting only one paragraph or your quotation is taken from the middle of a paragraph, do not indent the additional three spaces.

3. If you quote, paraphrase, or summarize material *already being quoted* in another source, use the abbreviation *qtd. in* (MLA) or *cited in* (APA) to clarify the actual source:

   Original: Baseball has mounted a campaign to stop pitchers from doctoring balls. It started when umpires sent several baseballs Joe Niekro had allegedly scuffed to American League president Bobby Brown. Brown's conclusion? "Those balls weren't roughed up; they were borderline mutilated," he said.

   Gammons, Peter. "O.K., Drop That Emery Board." *Sports Illustrated* 17 Aug. 2010: 34-36. Print.

   Student version (MLA): Pitchers have been cheating for as long as baseball has been played, and the controversy over Minnesota's Joe Niekro has done little to help pitchers' reputations. As American League president Bobby Brown notes, "Those balls weren't roughed up; they were borderline mutilated" (qtd. in Gammons 36).

4. Placement of end punctuation with direct quotations often confuses writers. It is particularly troublesome because the conventions are slightly

different for short quotations and long quotations (block format).

Short quotations.   With short quotations (and paraphrases and summaries), the period always follows the parenthetical documentation:

MLA: . . . the number of casualties" (81).

APA: . . . the number of casualties" (p. 81).

If the quoted sentence ends in something other than a period (exclamation or question mark), retain the punctuation *before* the quotation marks, and include an additional period after the parenthetical documentation:

MLA: . . . numbers were astronomical!" (82).

. . . could anyone tell?" (102).

APA: . . . numbers were astronomical!" (p. 82).

. . . could anyone tell?" (p. 102).

Long quotations (block format).   Because quotation marks are not used with block format (see rule 2), retain the end punctuation of the quoted material and simply add the parenthetical documentation without an additional period:

MLA: . . . the number of casualties. (81)

. . . numbers were astronomical! (82)

. . . could anyone tell? (102)

APA: . . . the number of casualties. (p. 81)

. . . numbers were astronomical! (p. 82)

. . . could anyone tell? (p. 102)

The sample essays in sections SP-1, SP-2, and SP-3 provide examples of correctly punctuated short and long quotations.

5. No lead-ins or commas are necessary when you are quoting only a word or a short phrase that can be integrated into your sentence:

MLA: In many folk songs of Norway, the people sing of their "fond devotion" for the land that "looms storm-scarred o'er the ocean" (Bjorn 31).

APA: . . . for the land that "looms storm-scarred o'er the ocean" (Bjorn, 2013, p. 31).

6. If you place a lead-in between two quoted sentences, follow it with a period:

MLA: "The play begins with almost Wagnerian intensity," observes director Betty Evans. "It suits the characters' temperament perfectly" (27).

APA: "The play begins with almost Wagnerian intensity," observes director Betty Evans (2013). "It suits the characters' temperament perfectly" (p. 27).

or

. . . director Betty Evans. "It suits the characters' temperament perfectly" (2013, p. 27).

7. If you place the lead-in at the end of a quotation that is a question or an exclamation, keep the original end punctuation and do not use a comma to set off the lead-in:

MLA: "Is there any solution to the annihilation which cold war encourages?" Davidson asks (31).

"The difference between the almost-right word and the right word is really a large matter—it's the difference between the lightning bug and lightning!" insists Mark Twain in his essay about writing (1).

APA: . . . war encourages?" Davidson asks (2012, p. 31).

. . . and lightning!" insists Mark Twain (1870) in his essay about writing (p. 1).

8. Use single quotation marks to set off quotations or titles of short works that are within material already set off with quotation marks:

MLA: Critic John Guest states, "The genius of Oscar Wilde can be found in short stories such as 'The Sphinx without a Secret' when one character says, 'Women are meant to be loved, not understood' " (15).

APA: Critic John Guest (2008) states, "The . . . understood' " (p. 15).

9. An ellipsis, which is three spaced periods (. . .), is used to indicate that you are omitting part of a direct quotation. Beginning writers often overuse this mark of punctuation, placing it at the beginning and end of every direct quotation. It is necessary to use an ellipsis *only* if the material is omitted from the middle of a passage or if, by omitting material at the beginning or the end, the quotation seems to be an unaltered sentence. Single words or phrases do not need ellipsis points. The following samples are in MLA format.

Ellipsis in the Middle

According to psychologist Donald Hurston, "Some dreams work almost like poems . . . offering uncanny distillations of the dreamer's emotions" (92).

Ellipsis at the End

According to psychologist Donald Hurston, "Dreams sublimate the process of wish fulfillment . . ." (92).

Ellipsis points that come at the end of a question or an exclamation are placed before the question mark or exclamation point:

Commodities expert Daniel Steele asks, "Will the Wall Street of the future be located in Japan . . . ?" (12).

Ellipsis to Indicate the Omission of the Last Part of a Sentence or One or More Complete Sentences

Harry Fiss, professor of psychiatry at Harvard, disagrees with the Freudian interpretation of dreams: "There is no need to assume dreams have a latent content. . . . Dreams simply continue the conscious concerns of waking life" (56).

If the omission occurs at the end of a sentence, use four spaced periods—three for the ellipsis and one for the final period.

10. When documenting well-known poems or verse plays, do not use page numbers. Since classic literary works are available in many different publications, it is more convenient for the reader merely to know the section (act, scene, part) and line. Works Cited and References entries should still cite page numbers.

Shakespeare's Hamlet insists he sees his father's ghost: "Why look you there! / My father in his habit as he lived" (3.4.135-36).

Anne Bradstreet's expressions of deep emotion are set against the stern background of Puritan New England: "My love is such that rivers cannot quench, / Nor aught but love from thee give recompense" (lines 7-8).

(For first citations, use the word "line" or "lines." For subsequent references, omit the word and just use line numbers.)

Direct Quotations: Activities

Q-4 Practice in Punctuating Quotations

Correctly punctuate and capitalize the following quotations using either MLA or APA format. When in doubt, refer to the rules for punctuating quotations in section Q-3. If you use the APA format, insert the publication date and the abbreviation for *page* or *pages*.

Example (MLA format)

"Diabetes more than doubles the risk of a disabling heart attack or stroke," claims medical writer J. Madeline Nash. "It is the leading cause of blindness in adults and accounts for a third of all cases of kidney failure" (52).

1. Can you hoodwink time and retard the aging process ask Bechtel and Waggoner   127

   For APA: publication date, 2012.

2. Quoted phrase: inevitably wrote with honesty, deliberation, and true emotion

Because Copland straddled popular and serious music, he had critics, but he succeeded because he inevitably wrote with honesty, deliberation, and true emotion Ames   57

For APA: publication date, 2013.

3. Make necessary corrections and, on the line, indicate the number of spaces to indent.

   In his book *Thailand,* Charles F. Keyes explains the results of Thailand's compulsory education system

   ___ the system of compulsory primary education has made Thailand's population one of the most literate in the world, even if a literacy rate of 93.2 percent in 1998 as reported in official statistics cannot be taken at face value. Compulsory education has also facilitated the participation of rural as well as urban people in the market economy and has given them access to written materials relevant to their economic lives   145

   For APA: publication date, 2009.

4. Another of Joyce's innovations says Stuart Gilbert is the extended use of the unspoken soliloquy or silent prologue, an exact transcription of the stream of consciousness of the individual   10

   For APA: publication date, 2008.

5. S. I. Hayakawa asks how, then, can we ever give an impartial report   41

   For APA: publication date, 2010.

6. Note that the author of the quotation is different from the author of the article. (*Hint:* See rule 3 in section Q-3.)

   The disappearance of drive-in movie theaters represents the loss of a significant part of American culture observes movie critic Pat Sondheim qtd. in Disch   94

   For APA: publication date, 2006. Use *cited in* rather than *qtd. in.*

7. Sociologist David MacNeil asserts a tidal wave of tourism has forced the Scottish people to abandon their native Gaelic language   139

   For APA: publication date, 2013.

8. Donald Katz states the image of self-fulfillment in a marriage where both partners work is hammered away by the reality of divorce statistics   183

   For APA: publication date, 2008.

9. There is indeed something disturbing, if not downright bogus claims children's author Malcolm Jones, Jr. about the idea that children must be tricked into the habit of reading with books designed just for them   62

   For APA: publication date, 2000.

10. In William Shakespeare's sonnet That Time of Year Thou Mayst in Me Behold the speaker compares his own aging process to the end of a day

    > In me thou see'st the twilight of such day
    > As after sunset fadeth in the west,
    > Which by-and-by black night doth take away,
    > Death's second self that seals up all in rest.
    >   lines 5–8

    For APA: publication date, 1609.

Q-5 Additional Practice in Punctuating Quotations

Correctly punctuate and capitalize the following quotations using either MLA or APA format. When in doubt, refer to the rules for punctuating quotations in section Q-3. If you use the APA format, insert the publication date and the abbreviation for *page* or *pages*.

Example (MLA Format)

"Does the poem 'Sunshine Enemies' reveal the intricacies of the human heart?" asks psychologist Wade Jennings (17).

1. Monroe asks is deregulation enough to eliminate the years of subsidies oil and natural gas have received   21

   For APA: publication date, 2013.

2. Current debates about educational policy have a fantasy quality to them suggests Hawley false premises lead to false promises   156

   For APA: publication date, 2005.

3. Quoted phrase: enmeshed in the web of the universe

   (*Hint:* See rule 5 in section Q-3.)

   The legends and myths of the Pueblo Indians are enmeshed in the web of the universe and pulsate with both animate and inanimate life forms Erdoes   11

   For APA: publication date, 2013.

4. Are we willing to accept as inevitable the extinction of nearly 200 animal species each year asks Hollister   15

   For APA: publication date, 2008.

5. History is not so much what actually happened historian Ronald Zoll claims but what people *believe* to have happened in the past   525

   For APA: publication date, 2002

6. Edgar Allan Poe widened the notions of fictional insanity with his short story The Tell-Tale Heart claims John Elfenbein   32

   For APA: publication date, 1978.

7. Van Dyk, author of the book *In Afghanistan,* states one of the world's great rivers, the Brahmaputra, begins as a glacial trickle in western Tibet and sweeps 1,800 miles to the Indian Ocean   372

   For APA: publication date, 2012.

8. On the line, indicate the number of spaces to indent.

   Professor Thomas Mack contends that the poem Wild Peaches parallels Elinor Wylie's life

   ___ her poem Wild Peaches offers insights into the carefully guarded secret of her abuse by a mentally deranged first husband, the excruciating experience of social ostracism after her elopement from this first marriage, and her eventual abandonment by her second husband   388

   For APA: publication date, 2009.

9. Note that the author of the quotation is different from the author of the article. (*Hint:* See rule 3 in section Q-3.)

   Medical experimentation on animals is necessary argues cancer researcher Richard Green to train surgeons, test vaccines, and make further medical progress qtd. in Levi   220

   For APA: publication date, 2005. Use *cited in* rather than *qtd. in.*

10. Literary critic Wayne Koestenbaum asks is the hysteria in Eliot's poem The Waste Land really as pathological as most readers think   118

    For APA: publication date, 2008.

Q-6 Practice in Creating Lead-Ins for Quotations

Using the quotations that follow, experiment with alternative methods of incorporating lead-ins. Follow the guidelines for punctuation and documentation presented in section Q-3 and prepare three versions of each quotation in either MLA or APA format. Place the lead-in or tag in all three positions: beginning, middle, and end. In preparing your lead-ins and documentation, refer to the publication and author information following each passage and compose lead-ins that establish the identity of the source. Publication information and the following examples are given in MLA format. (For examples in APA format, see section Q-2.)

Examples (MLA Format)

Lead-in at the beginning

English novelist and essayist Aldous Huxley asserts, "The advertisement is one of the most difficult of modern literary forms" (12).

Lead-in in the middle

"The advertisement," declares English novelist and essayist Aldous Huxley, "is one of the most difficult of modern literary forms" (12).

Lead-in at the end

"The advertisement is one of the most difficult of modern literary forms," writes Aldous Huxley, English novelist and essayist (12).

1. After Elvis Presley died on August 16, 1977, the number of Elvis tribute shows ballooned from an estimated 300 to over 3,000 nationwide.

   Soocher, Stan. *They Fought the Law: Rock Music Goes to Court.* New York: Schirmer, 2007. Print. (Quote is from page 11.)
   Stan Soocher is a law professor who represents celebrity musicians.

2. By the year 2050, whites will be a demographic minority but not a political or economic one.

   Chideya, Farai. "Shades of the Future." *Time* 1 Feb. 2006: 51-52. Print. (Quote is from page 51.)
   Farai Chideya serves as chair of the U.S. Committee for Racial Progress.

3. Travel writing is a good field for the new writer because much of the information needed to put together an article is often close at hand.

   Anderson, Robert. "So You Like to Write?" *Travel* 15 May 2008: 54+. Print. (Quote is from page 54.)
   Robert Anderson is the editor of *Travel* magazine.

4. Usually when the sun casts a warm glow in the early morning hours or toward the end of the day, the light wraps around and flatters the subject.

   Davis, Tim, and Renee Lynn. "Nature." *Popular Photography* Mar. 2013: 44-49. Print. (Quote is from page 46.)
   Tim Davis and Renee Lynn conduct nature photography seminars in national parks.

5. Adopting a positive habit like exercise can be as tough as breaking a bad one like smoking.

   This statement was made by Tanya Sommerfield, a trainer for the Olympic Men's Gymnastics Team, and was used in the following article. (*Hint:* Quoted in another source; see rule 3 in section Q-3.)
   Krocoff, Carol. "Just a Few Extra Steps Make All the Difference." *Los Angeles Times Online* 15 Feb. 2009: C4. *Proquest.* Web. 4 Mar. 2009.

Q-7 Practice in Integrating, Punctuating, and Documenting Quotations

From the information given about the source of each quotation, compose lead-ins that help to identify the author or source. Place the lead-in as cued, and rewrite the quotation and lead-in using either MLA or APA documentation. Publication information is in APA format.

1. Place lead-in at the beginning of the quote (*Hint:* Quoted in another source; see section Q-3, rule 3.)

   Wildlife officials want strict controls on importing and exhibiting exotic creatures to discourage trade that could further diminish their numbers in the wild.

   This statement was made by Mark Ellis, Director of the Bronx Zoo and quoted in the article cited below.

   Smothers, R. (2008, February 28). Scared of wild neighbors? *New York Times Online.* Retrieved from http://www.nytimes.com

2. Place the lead-in between two sentences.

   Credit cards are one of the primary battlegrounds on which you have to fight for your economic life. Those forces that are doing well in the current environment will do all they can to keep you locked into the borrow-and-spend lifestyle.

   Pollan, S., & Levine, M. (2007). *Die broke.* New York: Harper. (Quote is from page 146.)

   Stephen Pollan and Mark Levine have operated a successful financial consulting firm in New York for over twenty-five years.

3. Place the lead-in at the end.

Though Italians were frequently depicted as criminals, they were also often seen as comically hot-tempered waiters, barbers, or musicians.

Dooley, R. (2013, November 27). From Scarface to Scarlett. *Movie Critic,* 5–12. doi:10.352/s2773849movcrit3902_6 (The text retrieved from this Internet source does not have page numbers even though the original article is paginated.)

Roger Dooley is a noted author and movie critic.

4. Place the lead-in at the beginning. (*Hint:* Quoted in another source; see section Q-3, rule 3.)

Why Albuquerque, a city of 400,000, would need a full-time paramilitary unit is a question that should have been asked years ago.

This statement was made by Police Chief Jerry Galvin and quoted in the article cited below.

Egan, T. (2013, March 3). Armed for the drug war. *The Oregonian,* pp. A14–A16. (Quote is from page A16.)

5. Paraphrase the quotation, putting only select words or phrases in direct quotations. Place all the information for documentation in parentheses. Do not use a lead-in. (See section Q-3, rule 5.)

Employing techniques learned from Persia centuries ago, Kashmiri craftsmen operate over three thousand carpet looms and are capable of tying silk and woolen carpets whose quality rivals those of the Middle East.

Huyler, S. (2005). *Village India.* New York: Abrams. (Quote is from page 81.)

Q-8 Additional Practice in Integrating, Punctuating, and Documenting Quotations

From the information given about the source of each quotation, compose lead-ins that help to identify the author or source. Place the lead-in as cued and rewrite the quotation with the lead-in using either MLA or APA documentation and correct punctuation. Publication information is given in MLA format.

1. Create a full-sentence lead-in that comments on the ideas in the following lines of poetry written in 1807. Place the lead-in at the beginning and

use a colon. (*Hint:* Use block format and cite line numbers, not pages. See section Q-3, rule 10.)

The world is too much with us; late and soon,
Getting and spending, we lay waste our powers;
Little we see in Nature that is ours;
We have given our hearts away, a sordid boon!

Wordsworth, William. "The World Is Too Much with Us." *Literature: Reading Fiction, Poetry, Drama, and the Essay.* Ed. Robert DiYanni. McGraw-Hill, 1998. 703-04. Print. (Quote is from lines 1–4.)

William Wordsworth is a British poet known for his love of nature.

2. Place the lead-in between two sentences.

The show *Jeopardy!* never forces contestants to discover the "why" of a question. Therefore, it can be said that the show is both a cause and a symptom of the Information Age's lust for naked data.

Lidz, Franz. "What Is *Jeopardy?*" *Sports Illustrated* 1 May 2007: 94+. Print. (Quote is from page 94.)

Franz Lidz is the magazine's senior entertainment editor.

3. Place the lead-in at the end.

How many people know that Bette Midler dealt with poverty and racism when she was one of the few white kids in her Hawaiian school?

Simon, Clea. "Undaunted Women Inspire Listeners as Well as Hosts." *Boston Globe* 4 Mar. 2008. *ProQuest.* Web. 23 Mar. 2014.

Clea Simon is a staff writer.

4. Place the lead-in at the beginning.

History shows that choices expand—that new communications technologies and societal changes typically add more media rather than doom existing media.

Crawford, Walt. "New Niches for New (and Old) Media." *Online* July-Aug. 2008: 36-37. *Google Scholar.* Web. 15 Jan. 2014. (Quote is from page 36.)

Walt Crawford serves as Director of Research at Harvard.

5. Place a full-sentence lead-in at the beginning with a colon and use block format.

Like everyone else at the time, Jefferson believed in the Northwest Passage—a river, or a series of rivers connected by a short portage, that would cross the western mountains, make direct trade with the Orient easier and more profitable, and unlock the wealth of North America.

Duncan, Dayton. *Lewis and Clark: An Illustrated History.* New York: Knopf, 2013. Print. (Quote is from page 7.)

Dayton Duncan is a professor of history at the University of Texas.

Q-9 Common Errors in Citing Sources

1. Avoid redundancy in citation: if the author is mentioned in the lead-in, do *not* repeat the author's name in parentheses. If a parenthetical citation is necessary to mark the end of the source material and no page number is available, you can create a generic lead-in ("A recent article states") or a lead-in citing the title without the author's name and then use the author's name in parentheses.

   INCORRECT: **Sharon Begley, science editor of *Newsweek,* asserts, "The earth, the sea, and the air are the concern of every nation. Solutions must bridge the local and the global" (Begley).**

   CORRECT MLA: ***Newsweek's* science editor insists, "The earth, the sea, and the air are the concern of every nation. Solutions must bridge the local and the global" (Begley).**

   CORRECT APA: **A recent *Newsweek* article concludes, "The earth, the sea, and the air are the concern of every nation. Solutions must bridge the local and the global" (Begley, 2011).**

2. Observe the conventions of standard written English in the body of your paper even when the citation system uses nonstandard formatting for publication information, as with the "down style" of APA and CSE.

   INCORRECT: **In "How to stop being a drip" Charlene Dyson offers tips on water conservation (57).**

   In HOW TO STOP BEING A DRIP Charlene Dyson offers tips on water conservation (57).

   CORRECT MLA: **In "How to Stop Being a Drip" Charlene Dyson offers tips on water conservation (57).**

   CORRECT APA: **In "How to Stop Being a Drip" Dyson (2011) offers tips on water conservation (p. 57).**

3. Avoid wordiness and redundancy in lead-ins.

   INCORRECT: **According to the article "Global Warming," by Bryan Walsh it declares, "The U.S. produces nearly a quarter of the world's greenhouse gases" (12).**

   CORRECT MLA: **In "Global Warming," Bryan Walsh declares, "The U.S. produces nearly a quarter of the world's greenhouse gases" (12).**

   CORRECT APA: **In "Global Warming," Walsh (2013) declares, "The U.S. produces nearly a quarter of the world's greenhouse gases" (p. 12).**

4. Remember that "quotes" is what someone does when using the words of another person and is not a verb used in lead-ins.

   INCORRECT: **A quote by Brian Walsh argues, "The U.S. produces nearly a quarter of the world's greenhouse gases" (12).**

   In a recent *Newsweek* article Brian Walsh quotes, "The U.S. produces nearly a quarter of the world's greenhouse gases" (12).

   CORRECT MLA: **Bryan Walsh argues, "The U.S. produces nearly a quarter of the world's greenhouse gases" (12).**

   CORRECT APA: **Walsh (2013) declares, "The U.S. produces nearly a quarter of the world's greenhouse gases" (p.12).**

5. When quoting or paraphrasing the words of someone who is mentioned in a source but who is not the author of the source, remember to use "qtd. in" (MLA) or "cited in" (APA) in parenthetical citation.

   INCORRECT: **In his 1961 inaugural address John F. Kennedy asserts, "Science, technology, and education can be the ally of every nation" (Cooper).**

   CORRECT MLA: **In his 1961 inaugural address John F. Kennedy asserts, "Science, technology, and education can be the ally of every nation" (qtd. in Cooper).**

   CORRRECT APA: **In his 1961 inaugural address John F. Kennedy asserts, "Science, technology, and education can be the ally of every nation" (cited in Cooper, 2013).**

6. It is up to each writer to select and phrase the source information that is placed in a narrative lead-in, but information that is placed in parenthetical citation must follow the conventions of the documentation system exactly. For example, APA uses "p." before page numbers whereas MLA does not.

INCORRECT: Because of increasing warmer temperatures the Interior Department classified polar bears as a threatened species in 2006 (Nancy Gibbs, "The Truth about Denial," *Newsweek,* 22–29).

CORRECT MLA: The recent *Time* article "The Truth about Denial" notes that warmer temperatures caused the Interior Department in 2006 to classify polar bears as a threatened species (Gibbs 25).

CORRECT APA: The recent *Time* article "The Truth about Denial" (2013) notes that warmer temperatures caused the Interior Department in 2006 to classify polar bears as a threatened species (Gibbs, p. 25).

7. All direct quotations require narrative lead-ins.

INCORRECT: "Algae oil could be the fuel of the future" (Kertz 28).

CORRECT MLA: "Algae oil could be the fuel of the future," states Glen Kertz, principal scientist for Ventigro Energy (28).

CORRECT APA: G. Kertz (2012) predicts, "Algae oil could be the fuel of the future" (p. 28).

SELF-TEST

The following sentences all have errors in punctuation or formatting. On a separate sheet of paper rewrite each sentence carefully in full, making the necessary corrections. Although the sentences are written in MLA, you can choose either MLA or APA for your corrections. If using APA, assume the publication date is 2013.

1. Donald Grey asks, "Is there any solution to the devastation global warming will cause? (Grey 34)."

2. In the book *Romance is Illusion* by Carl Zimmer it states, "Love is pure magic." (120)

3. "Voters sense that politics is an act" (Joe Klein, pg. 72).

4. Barack Obama explains, "I am the son of a man from Kenya and a woman from Kansas" (Barnes).

5. Mark Tolson quotes "we live in techno-enthusiastic times."

Note: To check your answers turn to the answer key near the back of the book.

W-1 MLA and APA

Scholarly tradition has produced two basic styles for listing works at the end of a paper. Scholars in the humanities prefer the format prescribed by the Modern Language Association (MLA). Writers in business, social science, and natural science prefer the formats prescribed by the *Chicago Manual,* the American Psychological Association (APA), or the Council of Science Editors (CSE). The main differences between MLA and APA style can easily be seen in the following examples:

MLA:

Morgan, Robert. *Defining the Self in Society.* Orlando: Harcourt, 2013. Print.

Kerek, Marcel, and George Miller. "Campus Racism: Seeking the Real Victim." *Time* 21 Nov. 2012: 27-33. Google Scholar. Web. 7 July 2013.

APA:

Morgan, R. (2013). *Defining the self in society.* Orlando: Harcourt.

Kerek, M., & Miller, G. (2012, November 21). Campus racism: Seeking the real victim. *Time,* 27–33. Retrieved from http://www.kermil .com/RAC/2002.pdf

The two formats differ in the following ways:

1. The MLA spells out the full names of authors, whereas the APA uses initials for first and middle names and inverts the order of all names.
2. The MLA puts the publication date at the end of the entry, whereas the APA puts it immediately after the author's name.
3. The MLA uses standard capitalization for all titles, whereas APA uses a "down" style—only first letters and proper nouns are capitalized. The APA does use standard capitalization for journal titles, however.
4. The MLA places quotation marks around article titles, whereas the APA does not.
5. The MLA abbreviates months with more than four letters, whereas the APA does not.
6. For electronic sources MLA includes the date of access but omits the URL, while APA omits the date of access but includes the URL or DOI (if available).

Other differences between the MLA and APA styles will be explained in the exercises in section W-4. Also, for updates on citing electronic information, visit the MLA "Style Citations of Electronic Sources" site at <http://owl.english.purdue.edu>. For APA, visit <http://www.apastyle.org>.

A Word about Online Formatting Tools: Online formatting tools such as <http://citationmachine.net> can be a big help in getting a start on the basic formatting of source material. They can generate citations that can then be pasted into Works Cited and References pages. However, these software systems do not pick up all of the circumstances that may determine correct formatting because of the many different characteristics in information sources. You should *always* check a generated citation with the latest guidelines as explained in this text or online at the MLA and APA sites.

W-2 General Guidelines

One of the first steps in research is putting together a list of sources on a topic—a working bibliography. At first your sources should be written on note cards so that they can be easily shuffled and rearranged in alphabetical order as you add and drop items. Eventually you will need to arrange your sources into a "Works Cited" (MLA) or "References" (APA) list for the final draft of your paper. The information that you include about each source will be slightly different, depending on the type of source—computer database, book, journal, newspaper, interview, and so on. The easiest way to make sure that your information is complete and accurately formatted is to have on hand samples of entries from the documentation system you are using. The exercises in section W-4 include sample entries in MLA and APA format for most types of sources you will ever use. *Also, the samples Works Cited and References pages on pages 76–79 can serve as a handy reference.*

GUIDELINES

1. Alphabetize your list of entries according to the last name of the first author (or title if there is no author).

2. Ignore articles (*a, an, the*) when alphabetizing works by title, and, for MLA style, omit them entirely in the names of newspapers and magazines (for example, *New York Times, New Yorker*).

3. The first line of an entry begins at the left margin, and subsequent lines are indented five spaces in MLA and APA styles. (Notice that this "hanging indentation" is the opposite of usual paragraph indentation.) For example:

Santiago, Phillip. "Integrative Medicine: The Olympic Games Model." *Total Health* 4 Jan. 2011: 44-45. *Ebscohost.* Web. 22 Jan. 2013.

4. Double-space between entries and between lines of the same entry.

5. If several cities are listed for the place of publication, give only the first.

6. When listing the publisher, give only the important words, omitting first names, articles, business abbreviations, and descriptive words (for example, *John Wiley & Sons, Inc.* becomes *Wiley*).

7. For MLA, indicate *University Press* with the abbreviation *UP* (for example, *Cambridge University Press* becomes *Cambridge UP*).

8. Other examples of the correctly shortened format for publishers' names:

Harry N. Abrams, Inc.	Abrams
Dell Publishing Co., Inc.	Dell
Houghton Mifflin Co.	Houghton
D. C. Heath and Co.	Heath
Little, Brown, and Co.	Little
Oxford University Press	Oxford UP (MLA)
University of California Press	U of California P (MLA)

9. Within citations, follow periods with only one space.

10. In MLA style, abbreviate all months except May, June, and July (for example, *March 14, 2014,* becomes *14 Mar. 2014*).

11. When citing articles, include page numbers for the *entire* article. Do not give only the number of the page you may have used in your paper. That page number should appear in the text citation. Books do not require page numbers in a Works Cited or References list unless only a specific chapter is cited.

12. If a newspaper or periodical article runs more than one page, but the pages are not consecutive (that is, the article may be interrupted on page 34 and continued on pages 60–62), include only the first page and a plus sign when using MLA style (for example, 34+). For APA style, list all page numbers on which the article appears and include the abbreviations *p.* or *pp.* for newspaper, encyclopedia, and edited works (for example, pp. 34, 60–62).

W-3 Citing Electronic Information

Electronic entries in a Works Cited or References list begin with the same information that would be cited for a printed source, with additional information about the electronic source placed at the end. When citing online material in MLA style, include the date you accessed it (in addition to the publication date). If the publication date or page numbers are not available, use the abbreviations n.d and n. pag. When citing electronic material in APA style, do not include the date you accessed it unless the site is likely to change or no publication date is available (n.d.), but do give the network address, which is also called the uniform resource locator (URL). Scholarly journals in the sciences and social sciences now provide a DOI number (digital object identifier) similar to the ISBN for books. Include the DOI instead of the URL if it is available.

Online Databases

Since online databases usually have print equivalents, give information in the appropriate print format and then add the information about the electronic source. For MLA: name of database, medium of publication (Web), and date of access. For APA: Use the phrase *Retrieved from* and then give the URL or simply list the DOI if it is available. For example:

Retrieved from http://www.m-w.com/dictionary

Or

doi:10.2672/2283-000

Make line breaks in a URL only at slash marks or other punctuation: *before* the slash with APA and *after* the slash with MLA.

NOTE: **Because of the changing nature of electronic sources, documentation methods are still evolving. It is always a good idea to consult your instructor, librarian, and/or the web addresses that include updates.**

MLA AND APA UPDATES FOR DOCUMENTING ELECTRONIC SOURCES

For MLA: <http://owl.english.purdue.edu>

For APA: <http://www.apastyle.org/>

Works Cited and References: Activities

W-4 Practice in Punctuating MLA Works Cited

Insert the missing punctuation in the following MLA Works Cited page. Use underlining to indicate italics. When in doubt refer to the Sample MLA Entries at the end of the book. Selected answers are provided near the back.

Works Cited

Alexander, Jenni   Batik on Film   *Journal of Visual Arts* 3 (2008): 122-34   Web   1 June 2013

"An Analysis of Worker Drug Use and Workplace Policies and Programs"   National Opinion Research Center   20 July 2013   Web   7 Sept 2013

Atwan, Robert   Foreword   The Best American Essays   By Elizabeth Hardwick. New York: Ticknor, 2006   9-15   Print

Brown, Serjom   International Relations in a Changing Global System   New York: Westview, 2013   Print

Climate Change   *Compton's Online Encyclopedia*   Compton's 2012 ed. Web   14 July 2013

Eiler, John H., W. Gregory Wathen, and Michael R. Pelton   "Reproduction in Black Bears in the Southern Appalachian Mountains"   Journal of Wildlife Management 53.2 (2006): 353-360   Print

Kemorick Edward   Reclaiming a Sacred Past for Future Generations   *Billings Gazette Online* 23 Mar. 2009 Web   30 Apr 2013

Reir Sharon   Today's Money Markets   *Financial World* 11 July 2007: 56-59. Print.

Shepp, Archie.   Junebug Graduates Tonight   *Black Drama Anthology*. Eds. Woodie King and Ron Milner   New York: Columbia UP, 2002. 33-75   Print

Titanic   Dir. James Cameron. Perf. Leonardo DiCaprio and Kate Winslet   Paramount Pictures, 1997   Film

W-5 Practice in Punctuating APA References

Insert the missing punctuation in the following APA References page. Use underlining to indicate italics. When in doubt refer to the Sample APA Entries at the end of the book. Selected answers are provided near the back.

References

Alexander, J.   2008 Batik on film   Journal of Visual Arts, *3*, 122–134. Retrieved from http://www.press .uillinois.edu/journals/var.html

Atwan, R.   2006   Foreword. In E. Hardwick, *The best American essays.* (pp. 9–15). New York: Ticknor.

Brown, S   2013   *International relations in a changing global system*   New York   Westview

Eiler, J., Wathen, W. G., & Pelton, M. R.   2006 April   Reproduction in black bears in the southern Appalachian mountains   Journal of Wildlife Management, *53*(2), 353–360.

Kemorick E   2009, March 23   Reclaiming a sacred past for future generations   Billings Gazette Online   Retrieved from http://www.billingsgazette.com

National Opinion Research Center   2013   An analysis of worker drug use and workplace policies and programs   Chicago

Reir S   2007, July 11   Today's money market   *Financial World*   56–59

Shepp, A.   2002   Junebug graduates tonight   In W. King & R. Milner (Eds.), *Black drama anthology* (pp. 33–75). New York   Columbia University Press

South Dakota   2009   Compton's encyclopedia   (Vol. 25, pp. 4–8) New York: Collier's

Van Till, H. J.   2013   The creation: intelligently designed or optimally equipped   *Theology Today, 55,* 344–364

W-6 Sample Works Cited and References with Exercises (Electronic Sources)

When you are ready to prepare your list of sources, headed "Works Cited" (MLA) or "References" (APA), use the following sample entries as guides. After each sample entry you will find an exercise that will give you practice arranging sources in either MLA or APA style. Put your answers on a separate sheet. Complete listings of sample electronic sources for MLA and APA are given at the back of the book (pages 93 and 91).

Electronic Material from Online Sources

1. Scholarly Article from a Library Subscription Database

   MLA: Miller, Thomas R. "Interview with Marc Micozzi." *Health World,* 53.3 (2012): 17-20. EBSCOhost. Web. 27 Jan. 2013.

APA: Miller, T. (2012). Interview with Marc
         Micozzi. *Health World.* *53*(3), 17–27.
         doi:1156710.37653/0002

Note: For APA if a DOI (Digital Object Identifier) is available, use it rather than a URL.

EXERCISE 1

An article in the *International Journal of Business,* volume 34, issue 6, titled "Financing Higher Education" by Irwin Hyman, appeared in 2012 on pages 30–32. It was retrieved from the service *ProQuest Direct* on today's date. The DOI for the article is 1628282.22293/33392

2. Online Newspaper Article

MLA: Glazier, Lawrence. "Arbitrary Values and
         Contemporary Music." *New York Times
         on the Web.* New York Times, 5 Apr.
         2012: 4-5. Web. 18 Aug. 2013.

APA: Glazier, L. (2012, April 5). Arbitrary values
         and contemporary music. *New York
         Times on the Web,* pp. 4–5. Retrieved
         from http://nytimes.com/AP-values
         /html

EXERCISE 2

A June 12, 2012, article by Karen Rivedal titled "Living on the Edge" was retrieved on today's date from *New York Times on the Web* at <http://www.nytimes.com/library/tech/99/20>. It appeared on pages D12–13. The sponsor of the web site is the New York Times.

3. Blog

MLA: Fuentes, Phyllis. "Ozone and Our Future."
         Seattle Times. SeattleTimes.com, 16
         May 2008. Web. 13 July 2008.

APA: Fuentes, P. (2008, 16 May). Ozone and
         our future. *The Seattle Times.* Message
         posted to http://SeattleTimes
         .com_16may08//ozone

EXERCISE 3

On January 3, 2009, James Niven posted the article "Origins of Islam" to the *Yakima Valley Herald* at YVHerald.com. You accessed it on today's date. The URL is <http://www.yvherald.com_3jan09//origins>.

4. Wiki

MLA: "Chimpanzees." *Wikipedia.* Wikipedia
         Foundation, n.d. Web. 14 Jan. 2009.

APA: Chimpanzees. (n.d.). *Wikipedia.* Retrieved
         January 14, 2009, from http://www
         .chimpanzees.com/wiki/Wikipedia
         _Found

Note: For APA include access date if no publication date is available.

EXERCISE 4

The *Wikipedia* article "Tidal Waves" was accessed on today's date at <http://www.tidalwaves/com/wiki/wikipedia_found>. The sponsor of the site is the Wikipedia Foundation. There was no date available.

5. Google Scholar

MLA: McGann, David. "Pottery of Ancient
         Greece." *Classical Architecture* 43.2
         (2009): 32-40. *Google Scholar.* Web. 21
         Jan. 2009.

APA: McGann, D. (2009). Pottery of ancient
         Greece. *Classical Architecture, 43*(2),
         32–40. Retrieved from http://www
         .scholar.google.com//intl/en/pottery
         /greece/about.html

EXERCISE 5

The *Journal of Modern Psychology* article "Patterns of Behavior" by Elizabeth Goodall was accessed on today's date on *Google Scholar* at <http://www.scholar.google.com/intl/en/psych/goodall2008/about.html>. The article appeared in March 2008, in volume 46, issue 3, on pages 67–73.

6. Online Book

MLA: Dickens, Charles. *Our Mutual Friend.*
         London, 1863. *Project Gutenberg Etext.*
         Web. 13 April 2011.

APA: Dickens, C. (2001). *Our mutual friend.*
         (Original work published 1863).
         Retrieved from www.gutenberg.org
         /etext/884

EXERCISE 6

Charles Darwin published *The Expression of the Emotions in Man and Animals* in 1872. It was published on the Internet in 1997 and retrieved on today's date from www.gutenberg.org/dirs/etext98/

7. Report from a Web Site (no date)

MLA: "Wages and Benefits." Affirmative Action.
         n.d. Web. 5 July 2013.

APA: Wages and benefits. (n.d.). *Affirmative
         Action.* Retrieved on July 5, 2013, from
         www.affirmativeactionrespect.org

Note: APA includes retrieval date if no publication date is available.

EXERCISE 7

The web site *Southern History* posted a report with no date entitled "Battle of Olustee" at www.southern /history/olustee/org and was retrieved on today's date.

Electronic Material on CD-ROM

8. CD-ROM Articles
MLA: Bruner, Gerald. "Economic Forecast for the 21st Century." *Harvard Business Review* 42.4 (2004): 140-52. *ABI-Inform Ondisc.* CD-ROM.

APA: Bruner, G. (2004). Economic forecast for the 21st century. *Harvard Business Review, 42*(4), 140–152. Retrieved From UMI-Proquest File *(Abi-Inform Ondisc,* CD-ROM, March 2011 Release, Item 72432).

EXERCISE 8

An article by Barbara Newmans titled "Changing Roles in Managing Interns in the Workplace" was published in the *New York Times* on June 7, 2005. It appeared on page C-4. It was accessed through a CD-ROM database titled *New York Times Ondisc* distributed by UMI-ProQuest (Boston) in April 2011. The item number is 79-201.

W-7 Sample Works Cited and References with Exercises (Non-Electronic Sources)

When you are ready to prepare your list of sources, headed "Works Cited" (MLA) or "References" (APA), use the following sample entries as guides. After each sample entry you will find two exercises that will give you practice arranging sources in either MLA or APA style. Put your answers on a separate sheet, and **remember to arrange each pair of entries alphabetically.**

Books

1. A Book by One Author
MLA: Stokes, Henry Scott. *The Life and Death of Yukio Mishima.* New York: Noonday, 2013. Print.

APA: Stokes, H. S. (2013). *The life and death of Yukio Mishima.* New York, NY: Noonday.

EXERCISE 1

HarperBusiness in New York published Frank Rose's book, *The Agency* in 2005.

In 2004, Robert Munson wrote a book titled *Favorite Hobbies and Pastimes,* which was published by the American Library Association, a Chicago publisher.

2. Two or More Books by the Same Author
MLA: MacLaine, Shirley. *It's All in the Playing.* Toronto: Bantam, 2005. Print.
---. *My Lucky Stars.* New York: Bantam, 2007. Print.

MLA format: Alphabetize by title when listing more than one work by the same author. Rather than repeating the author's name, use three hyphens followed by a period.

APA: MacLaine, S. (2005). *It's all in the playing.* Toronto, Ontario: Bantam.
MacLaine, S. (2007). *My lucky stars.* New York, NY: Bantam.

APA format: List publications by the same author in the order of the year published, the earliest first. If two or more works by the same author have the same publication date, arrange them alphabetically by title and place lowercase letters after the year to identify sources cited in the text, for example, 2008a, 2008b.

EXERCISE 2

Michael R. Preiss wrote a book that was published in 2002 by Dell Publishing in New York. The book is titled *The Ultimate Dracula.*

In 2001 Preiss wrote *The Ultimate Werewolf,* which was published by Dell Publishing in New York.

3. A Book by Two or Three Authors
MLA: Engelmayer, John E., Jerome Davidson, and Robert M. Wagman. *Lord's Justice.* Garden City: Anchor, 2003. Print.

MLA format: Authors are listed in the order in which they appear on the title page of the book. The first author is listed by last name, first name, and any initials. Subsequent authors are listed in the standard first-name, last-name order.

> *APA:* Engelmayer, J. E., Davidson, J., & Wagman, R. M. (2003). *Lord's justice.* Garden City, NY: Anchor.

APA format: All authors are listed last name first followed by initials only. Note the use of the ampersand (&) rather than the word *and.*

EXERCISE 3

Loud and Clear was published in 2007 by Addison Wesley Longman in Reading, MA. This book was written by George L. Morrisey, Thomas L. Sechrest, and Wendy B. Warman.

The Phytoseiidae as Biological Control Agents of Pest Mites and Insects, published in 2006 by the University of Florida in Gainesville, was written by Tuomas S. Kostiainen and Marjorie A. Hoy.

4. A Book by Four or More Authors
> *MLA:* Kendall, Thomas, et al. *The Amber Wars and the Development of Europe.* New York: Shirlington, 2014. Print.

MLA format: If there are four or more authors or editors of a book, you may give only the first name listed followed by et al., a Latin abbreviation for "and others," or you may list all authors' names.

> *APA:* Kendall, T., Sutherland, W., Feinstein, R., & Randolph, E. (2014). *The amber wars and the development of Europe.* New York, NY: Shirlington.

APA format: All names are listed, as shown.

EXERCISE 4

In 2004, Jennifer Amers, Buddy Miles, Joan Summerfield, and Joyece Cameron wrote *Planting by the Cycles of the Moon* published by Sylvan Group of Boise, Idaho.

Mark Rollins, Charles Dunstan, Marjorie Bennett, and Hadley S. Phelps wrote *Trends of Geopolitical Evolution.* It was published in 2009 by McGraw-Hill, Inc., in New York.

5. A Book with One or More Editors
> *MLA:* Wertheimer, Neil, and Jack Croft, eds. *The Encyclopedia of Men's Health.* Emmaus: Rodale, 2014. Print.

> Marksbury, Richard A., ed. *The Business of Marriage.* Pittsburgh: U of Pittsburgh, 2004. Print.

> *APA:* Wertheimer, N., & Croft, J. (Eds.). (2014). *The encyclopedia of men's health.* Emmaus, PA: Rodale.
> Marksbury, R. A. (Ed.). (2004). *The business of marriage.* Pittsburgh, PA: University of Pittsburgh Press.

EXERCISE 5

Editors Michael T. Martin and Grace Cray compiled the book *New Latin American Cinema,* which was published in 2007 by Wayne State University Press in Detroit.

In 2006, John Sutherland edited a book, *The Oxford Book of English Love Stories,* which was published in Oxford by Oxford University Press.

6. A Work in an Anthology
> *MLA:* Hillerman, Tony. "Chee's Witch." *Popular Fiction.* Ed. Gary Hoppenstand. New York: Longman, 2012. 548-54. Print.

> *APA:* Hillerman, T. (2012). Chee's witch. In G. Hoppenstand (Ed.), *Popular fiction* (pp. 545–554). New York, NY: Longman.

EXERCISE 6

The essay "Suicide Is Not an Individual Right," by Robert P. George and William C. Proth, Jr., can be found on pages 24–32 in *Perspectives on Death,* edited by David L. Bender. This book was published by Greenhaven Press of New York in 2008.

The speech "Inaugural Address," by George Bush, can be found on pages 424–455 in *The Inaugural Addresses of the Presidents,* a 2007 publication of Gramercy in New York. The book was edited by John Gabriel Hunt.

7. An Introduction, Preface, Foreword, or Afterword
> *MLA:* Scanlan, Lawrence. Introduction. *The Man Who Listens to Horses.* By Monty Roberts. New York: Random. 2007. xiii-xlii. Print.

MLA format: If the author of the book is different from the person who wrote the preface, foreword, or afterword, give the author's full name, preceded by the word *By,* after the title of the book. If the author is the same person, give the last name only.

APA: Scanlan, L. (2007). Introduction. In M. Roberts, *The man who listens to horses* (pp. xiii–xiii). New York, NY: Random.

EXERCISE 7

Richard Aubry, M.D. wrote a foreword for *What to Expect When You're Expecting,* a book by Arlene Eisenberg, Heidi E. Murkoff, and Sandee E. Hathaway, which was published in 2006 by Workman Publishing in New York. His foreword appears on pages xvii–xix.

Alfred Kazin wrote an afterword for *The Adventures of Huckleberry Finn,* published in 2001 by Bantam in Toronto. The book was written by Mark Twain. Kazin's afterword appears on pages 282–292.

Articles

A note on pagination: Many scholarly journals paginate continuously from the first issue of each year through the last issue. (If the first issue ends on page 206, the second issue will begin on page 207.) Such journals are often highly specialized and deal with a limited range of topics. The *James Joyce Quarterly,* for example, will have articles on the life and works of James Joyce only. The *Journal of Learning Disabilities* is limited to a specialized area in the field of education. By numbering pages continuously, these journals emphasize the continuity of thought from one issue to the next in a particular year.

Most magazines and general-interest journals begin each issue with page number 1. The subject matter of these periodicals will cover a wider range of topics, and each issue may be quite different in content from other issues; thus, continuous pagination would be inappropriate.

8. *An Article in a Continuously Paginated Journal*
MLA: Magee, Jeffrey. "Revisiting Style and Form in 'Copenhagen.' " *Journal of American Musicological Society* 68.2 (2004): 42-66. Print.

MLA format: Include volume number, issue, and year.

APA: Magee, J. (2004). Revisiting style and form in "Copenhagen." *Journal of American Musicological Society, 68,* 42–66.

APA format: Capitalize the main words of all periodical titles and put them and the volume number in italics. Notice that only the first word in an article title (along with proper nouns) is capitalized. For newspaper articles, use the abbreviations p. and pp. to indicate page numbers. Omit these abbreviations in magazine and

journal entries. When citing electronic sources, include the issue number as well.

EXERCISE 8

"How Great a Good Is Virtue?" an article by Thomas Hurka, can be found in the Volume XCV, 2008 issue of *The Journal of Philosophy,* on pages 181–203.

Susan Balandin and Teresa Iocono published their article "A Few Well-Chosen Words" in the Volume 14, 2008 issue of *Augmentative and Alternative Communication,* on pages 147–161.

9. *An Article in an Individually Paginated Journal*
MLA: Kessler, Timothy P. "Political Capital: Mexican Financial Policy under Salinas." *World Politics* 51.1 (2005): 36-66. Print.

MLA format: Include volume number, issue, and year.

APA: Kessler, T. P. (2005). Political capital: Mexican financial policy under Salinas. *World Politics, 51*(1), 36–66.

APA format: If each issue begins on page 1, include the issue number (1), and remember to italicize the volume number: 51.

EXERCISE 9

In volume 20, issue number 3, of *Journal of American Culture,* published in 2007, Philip K. Jason wrote an article titled "Vietnamese in America: Literary Representations." It appeared on pages 43–50.

"How Do You Spell S(you)ccess?" an article published in February 2009 in volume 8, issue number 7, of *Children's Writer* on page 2, was written by Joan Broerman.

10. *An Article in a Monthly or Bimonthly Magazine*
MLA: Schuster, Angela M. H. "Colorful Cotton." *Archaeology* July-Aug. 2003: 40-45. Print.

APA: Schuster, A. M. H. (2003, July/August). Colorful cotton. *Archaeology, 48*(9), 40–45.

APA format: Remember to give volume number if specified.

EXERCISE 10

The article "The Full Energy Workout" by Rachel Schaeffer appeared in the January/February 1999 issue of *Natural Health* on pages 116–121.

In the February 2009 *Funny Times,* readers can find an article titled "Dates from Hell" by Victoria Jackson and Mike Harris on pages 6–7.

11. An Article in a Weekly or Biweekly Magazine

MLA: Taylor, Chris. "The History and the Hype." *Time* 18 Jan. 2004: 72-73. Print.

APA: Taylor, C. (2004, January 18). The history and the hype. *Time, 153,* 72–73.

EXERCISE 11

Diane McWhorter had the article "Since Mississippi Burned" published in the January 9, 2009, volume 32 issue of *People* on pages 36–50.

On pages 50–51 in the January 11, 2009, issue of *Forbes,* Michelle Conlin published her article "Mass with Class."

12. A Signed Article in a Newspaper

MLA: Vogel, Steve. "Marines Fault Pilot for Alpine Accident." *Washington Post* 9 Feb. 1999: A3. Print.

MLA format: Include the location of the newspaper in brackets if it is not included in the title or if it is not widely known (for example, **Post Intelligencer [Seattle]**). Also, if the newspaper published different editions, specify the edition following the date (for example, 20 Dec. 1988, late ed.: 7B.).

APA: Vogel, S. (1999, February 9). Marines fault pilot for alpine accident. *The Washington Post,* p. A3.

EXERCISE 12

Thomas Stultaford wrote an article titled "Americans Come Clean on How to Avoid Tummy Trouble," which appeared on page 11 of the January 28, 2009, issue of the *Seattle Times.*

The February 7, 2009, *The Philadelphia Inquirer* article "Minorities Want a Piece of Stadium Pie" was written by Howard Goodman and appeared on page B1.

13. An Unsigned Article in a Newspaper

MLA: "Toymaker Has Plans for Barbie at 40: A Hip Look, Including a Tattoo." *St. Louis Post-Dispatch* 4 Feb. 1999: A2. Print.

APA: Toymaker has plans for Barbie at 40: a hip look, including a tattoo. (1999, February 4). *St. Louis Post-Dispatch,* p. A2.

Both formats: In the text, use a shortened title for parenthetical documentation and omit page number with one-page articles—MLA: (**"Toymaker"**); APA: (**"Toymaker,"** 1999).

EXERCISE 13

In the January 30, 2009, issue of the *St. Petersburg Times,* the article "Jury Finds Teen Guilty of Murder" appeared on page 5B.

"Irwin Highlights Success with Hit" appears in the February 1, 2009, issue of *USA Today* on page 20C.

14. An Editorial in a Newspaper

MLA: Employers Can Limit Free Speech." Editorial. *San Francisco Chronicle* 5 Feb. 2003: 21. Print.

APA: Employers can limit free speech [Editorial]. (2003, February 5). speech. *San Francisco Chronicle,* p. 21.

EXERCISE 14

"Keep Virginia's Colleges Strong," an editorial, appeared in the February 9, 2009, issue of the *Washington Post* on page A16.

On February 1, 2009, *USA Today* ran the editorial "Potential Threat to Blood Supply Emerges, Demanding Caution" on page 14A.

Other Sources

15. A Government Document

MLA: United States. OECD Council. *Improving Ethical Conduct in the Public Service.* Washington: GPO, 2004. Print.

MLA format: For unsigned government documents, indicate the source (state, country, and organization) followed by the title, as just shown. Use the abbreviation GPO for Government Printing Office.

APA: OECD Council. (2004). *Improving ethical conduct in the public service.* Washington, DC: U.S. Government Printing Office.

EXERCISE 15

In 2007, the U.S. Department of Energy published a pamphlet titled *Nuclear Powerplant Safety: Source Terms.*

In 2008, the United States Air Force produced a pamphlet titled *Air Force Logistics,* which was published by the Government Printing Office in Washington, DC.

16. An Interview

MLA: Fields, Rick. "In Light of Death." Interview. By Helen Tworkov. *The Sun* Apr. 2004: 10-14. Print.

Bailey, Philip. Personal interview. 21 Dec. 2008.

Emory, Edward. Telephone interview. 14 Jan. 2008.

APA: Fields, R. (2004, April). In light of death [Interview with Helen Tworkov]. *The Sun*, pp. 10–14.

APA format: Personal interviews and telephone conversations such as those listed in MLA format are not recoverable and consequently are not included in the reference list for APA even though they are cited in the text:

Bailey (personal communication, December 21, 2008) states that the treatment of schizophrenia often requires drugs.

EXERCISE 16

Reuben Askew was interviewed by Jan Godown for the Spring 2008 issue of *Florida State University in Review*. The article, titled "A Talk with Reuben Askew," can be found on pages 34–39, 60–61.

To complete your research project on the Mayan civilization, you talked with Dr. David Aquino, professor of history, on January 17, 2014.

17. A Reference Work

MLA: Standen, Edith. "Lace." *The Encyclopedia Americana*. 2004 ed. Print.

MLA format: Encyclopedias and dictionaries require neither publication information nor page numbers because they are well known and the information is alphabetized. Little-known works, however, should include all publication information.

APA: Standen, E. (2004). Lace. *The encyclopedia Americana* (Vol. 16, p. 106). Danbury, CT: Grolier.

APA format: Include volume, page, and publication information for all encyclopedias and dictionaries.

EXERCISE 17

In the *Encyclopedia of Sleep and Dreaming*, Adrian Morrison published her article "Animals' Dreams" on page 223. The book was published by Macmillan in New York in 2008. No volume number was available.

"Lutherans" by Theodore Tappert appears in the 2005 edition of *Collier's Encyclopedia*, which is published by Collier's of New York. The article is in Volume 15 and can be found on pages 116–118.

18. An Unsigned Article in a Reference Work

MLA: "Noted American Cartoonists." *The World Almanac and Book of Facts*. 2003 ed. Print.

APA: Noted American cartoonists. (2003). In *The world almanac and book of facts* (Vol. 6, pp. 333–334). Matwah, NJ: World Almanac Books.

EXERCISE 18

An article titled "Jet Lag" can be found in the 2005 *World Book Medical Encyclopedia* published by Dell in New York. It is in Volume 7 on pages 507–508.

An article titled "Perfumes, Cosmetics, and Toiletries" appears in the volume 1, 2005 edition of *U.S. Industry Profiles*. This reference book is published by Gale Research Inc. in New York. The article appears on pages 414–420.

19. A Book or a Pamphlet by Corporate Authors

MLA: School of Public Affairs. *Report from the Institute for Philosophy and Public policy*. Baltimore: U of Maryland P, 2004. Print.

APA: School of Public Affairs. (2004). *Report from the institute for philosophy and public policy*. Baltimore, MD: University of Maryland Press.

EXERCISE 19

In 2007, the Commission on the Humanities published a report titled *The Humanities in American Life: Report of the Commission on the Humanities*. It was published in Berkeley by the University of California Press.

The Boston Women's Health Book Collective compiled a book titled *Our Bodies, Ourselves: A Book by and for Women*, which was published in 2006 by the New York publisher Simon & Schuster, Inc.

20. A Film or a Recording

MLA: *Armageddon*. Dir. Michael Bay. Perf. Bruce Willis, Billy Bob Thornton, and Liv Tyler. Touchstone, 1996. Film.

The Beatles. "Lucy in the Sky with Diamonds." *Sgt. Pepper's Lonely Hearts Club Band*. Apple Records, 1967. LP.

APA: Bruckheimer, J. (Producer), & Bay, M. (Director). (1996). *Armageddon* [Film]. Hollywood, CA: Touchstone.

The Beatles. (1967). Lucy in the sky with diamonds. On *Sgt. Pepper's Lonely Hearts Club Band* [record]. Hollywood: Apple Records.

APA format: Give the name and function of principal contributors to films and recordings.

EXERCISE 20

In your paper you refer to a song called "China Roses" by Enya. It comes from her compact disc *Paint the Sky with Stars,* which was produced in New York by Warner Music in 1997.

In your research paper about James Dean, you decide to quote the dialogue in a scene from the movie *Rebel Without a Cause.* It was directed by Nicholas Ray and in addition to James Dean starred Natalie Wood and Sal Mineo. It was distributed in 1955 by Warner Brothers of Los Angeles.

21. A Television or Radio Program

MLA: "Need More Vacation?" *CNN Crossfire.* Narr. Mike Kinsley, Pat Buchanan, John Zalvsky, and Fred Smith. CNN. 26 July 2001. Television.

"The Bottom Line." Narr. Linda Wertheimer. *All Things Considered.* Natl. Public Radio. WJCT, Jacksonville, FL. 10 Oct. 2008. Radio.

APA: York, J. (Producer). (2001, July 26). Need more vacation? In *CNN crossfire.* New York, NY: CNN.

Lexington, M. (Producer). (2008, October 10). The bottom line. In *All things considered.* National Public Radio. Jacksonville, FL: WJCT.

EXERCISE 21

A weekly PBS radio program titled *Mystery* featured "The Red-Headed League" on a Boston station, WGBH. The show, which was directed by Mary Sullivan, aired on February 15, 2006, and was narrated by Vincent Price.

John Thomas moderated a weekly television show titled *Meet the Challenge.* The episode "Progress in Duval County Public Schools" aired on the PBS network, WJCT in Jacksonville, Florida, on April 13, 2008.

W-8 Arranging a Works Cited or References List with Electronic Sources

Arrange the following electronic sources in correct MLA or APA format. **Remember to alphabetize the entries.**

1. The article "Inflation in Health Care" was first published in print in *Business Week* on March 12, 2001. The author is Samuel L. Miller and it appeared on pages 14–16. It was retrieved through *ProQuest* database on July 7, 2013, and the article's URL is <www.businessweek.com/2001/14/b47821.html>.

2. The article "Photography and Vision" was first published in print in *Photography* on April 17, 2000. The author is Sharon Lavani and it appeared on pages 45–48. It was retrieved through *EBSCOhost* database on January 5, 2014, and the URL was given only for the database: <http://ebsco14/rtw/4829/2001>.

3. The American Psychological Association is the sponsoring organization for a web site titled *How to Cite Information from the World Wide Web.* It was last updated June 20, 2013, and was retrieved on September 5, 2013, at <http://www.apa.org/journals/webref.html>.

4. The web site sponsor *Human Resource Center* published the article "Improving Employees' Performances" by David Farrar on October 17, 2000. It was 22 paragraphs long, and the paragraphs were numbered. It was retrieved on February 15, 2014, at <http://www.home.netscape/business/human resources.html>.

5. Steven Weisman published the article "Justice in the Courtroom" in *New York Times on the Web* on May 4, 2001. It was retrieved on Dialog database on October 20, 2013. The URL for the article is <http://nytimes.com/yr/mo/day/news/wwsun7.html>.

6. Jane Randal published the 2008 article "Peter Pan in America" in *American Folktales* on pages 35–43 in volume 32, issue 7. It was accessed on today's date on *Google Scholar* at <http://www.scholar/google.com/intl/en/peterpan/randal/about/html>.

SP-1 SAMPLE STUDENT RESEARCH PAPER IN MLA FORMAT WITH ANNOTATED BIBLIOGRAPHY

1″

Chauncey 1

Shanna R. Chauncey

Professor Chavez

English 103

5 January 2014

Traditional and Alternative: Health Care for the Future

As a doctor's daughter I learned early how conventional medicine works. In my own home the topic of illness never came up except if one of us contracted a cold, strep throat, flu, or the occasional childhood disease such as mumps. We knew the procedure from that point—a look at our throat, the quick touch on our foreheads to determine whether we had a fever and then the dreaded shot or pill. After that we spent a couple of days on the couch watching TV until we were no longer contagious. Although I knew my father was a highly respected and dedicated physician, I never got the feeling that he considered other factors that may or may not have contributed to our health. He openly scoffed at the mention of the few alternative approaches that somehow managed to enter the conversation at the dinner table, such as massage, chiropractic medicine, or acupuncture. As I got older, I began to wonder at my father's philosophy of medicine, which I discovered represented the typical doctor's thinking in America. He seemed very knowledgeable about the scientific aspects of his field. He regularly attended medical conferences and he stayed abreast of the current advances. But it seemed to me that his scientific expertise was spent treating the symptoms of illness, through either medicine or surgery, not determining the ultimate causes.

The questioning of conventional medicine that I began as a young woman mirrors the current questioning of our whole society. According to a report compiled by Dr. David Eisenberg of Boston's Deaconess Medical Center, 40% of the adult population seeks alternative medical care, making more visits to these practitioners than to medical doctors (qtd. in Cowley and Underwood). It is no longer good enough for many of us to wait until we get sick to obtain the healing pill or surgical procedure. We don't feel as comfortable in the submissive role as patient receiving orders from an all-knowing physician. The time has come for conventional practitioners to include alternative therapies in their

1″

1″

Double-space all text in 12-point Times New Roman font; do not single-space any part of the paper.

Title is centered in 12-point font without quotes, underlining, bold, or italics.

Indent ½″ ⟶

Personal anecdote creates interest and shows writer's purpose and connection to the topic. The public issue or thesis is clarified in second paragraph.

First time an author is mentioned, give first and last name and some additional identifying information. Although Eisenberg is being summarized, he is not the author of the article, thus the need for *qtd. in.* Note how source material is integrated into the discussion both before and after.

Thesis or controlling idea. (See section R-4 for details about how this thesis was developed.)

treatment plans because alternative medicine addresses the public's desire for holistic care, prevention, and guidance in how to establish a healthy lifestyle.

Specific details illustrate the topic of a typical visit to a doctor.

To illustrate, examine the following scenario and compare it to your last visit to a physician. Your appointment begins with a 30-minute wait with other sick and presumably contagious patients. You spend at least another 15 minutes in the examination room wearing a skimpy gown and staring at the walls. When your doctor arrives, she spends the first few minutes familiarizing herself with you by reading a checklist you completed two years ago about your medical history, medication allergies, and the two lifestyle items of whether you smoke and/or drink. She gives you a few minutes to describe your current problem and invariably, after glancing again at the checklist for your allergies to medicine, she prescribes an antibiotic or painkiller. End of visit. End of symptom. No more illness.

Specific details illustrate the topic of a visit to an alternative practitioner.

Contrast this experience with a typical visit to an alternative practitioner such as a massage therapist. Often their offices are much more comfortable and less crowded. A massage therapist devotes the first visit to familiarizing herself with the patient. Her checklist consists of questions spanning the entire breadth of a person's lifestyle. They will include inquiries about an individual's spiritual leanings, the levels of stress in his life, the kind of diet and exercise routines he follows, and the emotional ups and downs present in his everyday life. The therapist usually completes this extensive questioning to determine what sort of treatment will be best for this individual. She doesn't even assume that her therapy will be the one of choice and will admit up front that if the problem is, indeed, structural then actually a medical doctor would serve the patient's needs more efficiently. If treatment is indicated, then she focuses on patient self-education and self-help so that a person can go home and take measures to prevent problems and maintain health. In addition, she will recommend other treatments which may be blended to treat patients holistically.

Lead-in includes identifying information. Two-sentence summary/quote is framed with lead-in at the beginning and source credit in last sentence.

Medical doctors could easily approach their treatment plans similarly, but they would have to completely change the way that they view health. Dr. Burton Goldberg, author of *A New Understanding of Alternative Medicine,* states that currently doctors learn about organ systems as if they worked independently, not interdependently. Thus Goldberg believes the whole business of medicine in our country offers specialization in such areas as gynecology, orthopedics, and neurology but ignores the "intrinsic interrelatedness of all parts of our body and the complex dynamism of life forces." Most physicians, including my father, say

No page reference with this Internet source.

that it is a messy business dealing with a person's emotional or mental state in

Chauncey 3

Introduce long quotations with full-sentence lead-ins and a colon.

Use block format for quotations of more than four typed lines. With block format, the end punctuation comes before the parenthetical documentation.

Commentary sentence explains significance of quotation.

One-sentence summary with author and page citation.

Commentary sentence integrates previous summary.

Illustration has figure number, caption, and source information.

treating patients. Physicians say it is not their "area" and they don't feel qualified to delve into such personal matters. Dr. Andrew Weil of the University of Arizona College of Medicine describes his reaction to his own medical training:

> Most of the treatments I had learned in four years at Harvard Medical School and one of internship did not get to the root of disease processes and promote healing, but rather suppressed these processes or merely counteracted the visible symptoms of disease. I had learned almost nothing about health and its maintenance, about how to prevent illness—a great omission, because I have always believed that the primary function of doctors should be to teach people how not to get sick in the first place. (19)

Increasingly, people are beginning to demand the attentiveness that Weil describes. People want health care professionals to consider "the whole person" when they are treated. In her article "Complementary Health Care," holistic chiropractor Merri Harris defines a good practitioner as one who considers the physical, emotional, and spiritual aspects of a person's make-up (24). In Oriental medicine different energy centers of the body are called chakras and they are thought to keep the spiritual, mental, emotional, and physical health of the body in balance (see fig. 1). Clearly this whole-person approach should not be limited to those health specialists who practice outside mainstream medicine.

Fig. 1. This artist's conception shows the seven energy centers or chakras of the body. From Merri Harris, "Complementary Health Care," *Today's Health*, Nov. 2008: 25. Web. 14 Dec. 2008.

Student draws on personal experience to develop the topic.

The experience I have had in dealing with a serious back problem over the course of several years has proved to me the effectiveness of the holistic health approach. The muscle spasms and pain from which I suffered often rendered me unable to move or walk straight. My doctor's visits resulted in the predictable treatment of anti-inflammatory and muscle relaxant drugs and advice to stay in bed. It took me several years to realize that something more had to be done. I insisted on a different treatment plan from my doctor, at which point he ordered an MRI. The results revealed a structural problem, and my doctor referred me to a neurosurgeon. In our five-minute visit this doctor encouraged surgery and handed me a pamphlet that demonstrated five exercises I could do in the meantime. That was the end of my visit and the end of my reliance on mainstream medicine to help me with my problem. Certainly I would not minimize the help I received to that point. No alternative health care provider could have provided me with the diagnosis of such a technologically advanced test as an MRI. But mainstream medicine could not help me beyond that. My condition was not one that would just disappear with the proper medication, nor is back surgery always successful. Dr. John Hoey, Editor in Chief of *Canadian Medical Association Journal,* admits, "Any illness that we label 'chronic' can be viewed at least in part as one of conventional medicine's failures" (803). Chronic conditions often will respond favorably to alternative approaches, however.

Short quote with identifying information about the author and a follow-up sentence that integrates the quote and advances the thesis.

Personal anecdote supports thesis.

I chose to look elsewhere for help and I began by visiting a massage therapist. From him I learned that perhaps through a healthy lifestyle I could avoid further painful bouts with my back. I have begun enriching my diet with a wider variety of fruits, vegetables, and grains and I drink lots of water. I take a multivitamin/mineral supplement and practice a yoga program designed for people with back problems. I believe that these factors are responsible for my last two pain-free, incident-free years.

Details define and explain advantages of alternative approaches to health care.

Other examples of preventative therapies include Ayurvedic medicine, biofeedback, reflexology, Reiki, and herbal medicine. Even though these treatments may not be backed up by scientific evidence, they are commonly used by many people in our society who have experienced positive results with them in their lives. Nobody could say that meditation or a healthy diet could hurt someone. So why shouldn't doctors at least consider them as alternative treatments? Goldberg claims that again the fragmented approach of conventional medicine will have to change. As long as doctors make a living and are recognized for

Two-sentence paraphrase with frame. Last name only since Goldberg has been identified already.

Chauncey 5

This Internet site has no page number, so end frame is created with narrative source credit in last sentence. (Commentary sentence integrates paraphrase.)

Use full-sentence lead-ins with colon for long quotations.

Block format.

No page reference with this Internet source.

Follow-up discussion integrates long quotation and advances the thesis.

Two-sentence summary with frame (lead-in and page reference).

Summary. No page reference with one-page article. Discussion makes clear where summary ends. Commentary sentence integrates previous sources and advances the thesis.

"rescue" medicine, they will not place a lot of stock in such aspects of holistic health as prevention, asserts Goldberg. Alternative therapies have allowed me to gain some relief because they emphasize prevention rather than trying to fix the problem only after it has occurred.

The other important component of holistic medicine is maintenance of health through lifestyle choices. Like prevention, attention to everyday health problems is not a major element in conventional medicine. But a reasonable person would not deny that individuals' attitudes, feelings, values, and emotions all contribute to overall health. Including these aspects of a person's constitution in a treatment plan places the emphasis on health, not illness, the whole person, not isolated areas of the body. The practitioner might suggest transforming a patient's diet or suggest a whole different approach to exercise. These life-altering treatments return the responsibility for health to individuals. Taking responsibility for one's own health is as it should be, declares Dr. Marc Micozzi, executive director of the College of Physicians of Philadelphia:

> Health is something that must be pursued. It's a path that people have to choose to get on. They can't be given health with a pill or an operation. It goes even beyond lifestyle. It's an issue of philosophy, and every person really has to be responsible to stay healthy, and get well when they're sick, and has to focus on their ability to care for themselves.

Certainly taking such measures as reducing saturated fat or adding twenty minutes of exercise to our daily schedules constitutes positive beginning steps toward improving our well-being. But adopting a philosophy of health in daily living, as Micozzi suggests, takes time, dedication, and self-education. Such ancient systems as Chinese medicine, yoga, or Ayurvedic medicine embody whole systems of living. For example, in his book *Perfect Health*, Dr. Deepak Chopra explains that the Ayurvedic approach to health involves allowing the mind to communicate with the body at the deepest levels in order to bring first the mind then the body into balance. This is accomplished through meditation, diet, exercise, daily routines, and seasonal routines (93). Other systems of health might suggest different practices for maintaining optimum health. Dr. Julian Whitaker, director of Whitaker Wellness Institute, outlines the major focus of his treatments as diet, nutrition, and herbal supplementation. Like Micozzi and Chopra, he views health as a system for living. The point is that there is so much we can do in this area, so many goals worth aspiring to.

Chauncey 6

Nobody can discount the strides modern medicine has achieved in the areas of emergency and heroic care. But now it is time to seek ways to integrate mainstream and alternative medicine. Doctors such as Andrew Weil are working toward such ends.

As Weil points out, the University of Arizona trains doctors to initiate programs in integrative medicine (medicine that blends conventional practices with alternative approaches) in different areas of the country. In addition, doctors in the program are learning methods in such areas as herbal medicine and mind-body medicine (20). I think perhaps even my father will adopt a few alternative medical therapies. He is fascinated by my vegetarian diet and makes such comments as, "Give me an example of what you would fix for dinner." On recent visits home I have caught him in the basement doing a daily stint on a treadmill. He even succumbs to regular afternoon naps, his form of relaxation or meditation.

Maybe when doctors open themselves up to practicing prevention in their own lives they will see that proof lies in experience. Elsewhere, universities and hospitals are conducting research on alternative approaches to medicine. This commitment on the part of professional health care providers can only lead to a better educated public more devoted to taking responsibility for their own health. It is a win-win situation. Doctors put an end to their fragmented rescue approach to medicine and focus on teaching people how to stay healthy. Patients concentrate on helping themselves to better health. It is only with this hand-in-hand approach that health care providers and individuals can step to a healthy rhythm into the twenty-first century.

½"

1"

Chauncey 7

Works Cited

Chopra, Deepak. *Perfect Health*. New York: Harmony, 2013. Print.

Cowley, Geoffrey, and Anne Underwood. "What's Alternative?" *Newsweek* 11 Nov. 2008: 68. Print.

Goldberg, Burton. *The Burton Goldberg Home Page*. 3 Feb. 1998. The Burton Goldberg Group. Web. 27 Jan. 2009.

1"

Two-sentence summary with frame (lead-in and page reference).

Discussion integrates previous summary and advances the thesis.

Positive tone in conclusion suggests combining alternative and traditional approaches to health care.

Works Cited on a separate page.

Harris, Merri. "Complementary Health Care." *Today's Health* Nov. 2008:

24-33. Web. 14 Dec. 2008.

Hoey, John. "The Arrogance of Science and the Pitfalls of Hope." *Canadian*

Medical Association Journal 159 (2006): 803-04. Print.

Micozzi, Marc. "Interview with Marc Micozzi, M.D." *Health World Online* 20

Oct. 2008: 10-14. Web. 27 Jan. 2011.

Weil, Andrew. "Dr. Andrew Weil: Healer, Teacher, Visionary." Interview. By

Parris M. Kidd. *Trio* Feb.-Mar. 2008: 18-20. Print.

Whitaker, Julian. "Sparkling Eyes Got Me Started." *Health and Healing* 7.1

(2007): 1. Print.

½″ ↕

Chauncey 8

Annotated Bibliography on a separate page.

Annotated Bibliography

Chopra, Deepak. *Perfect Health*. New York: Harmony, 2013. Print. Explains in

detail the Ayurvedic system of health. Chopra is a well-known expert

on this ancient mind/body medicine. In fact, he has reached celebrity

status in the U.S., so his ideas regarding this very specific alternative ap-

proach to medicine would be credible with many readers.

Cowley, Geoffrey, and Anne Underwood. "What's Alternative?" *Newsweek* 11

Nov. 2008: 68. Print. Defines some of the more widely used alternative

approaches to medicine and discusses some recent studies that prove or

disprove the benefits of several unconventional forms of medicine such

as chiropractic and herbal supplementation. The article also contains an

important statistic regarding how many people in the U.S. use the ser-

vices of practitioners of alternative medicine.

Goldberg, Burton. *The Burton Goldberg Home Page*. 3 Feb. 1998. The Burton

Goldberg Group. Web. 27 Jan. 2009. Presents arguments against

conventional medicine's fragmented approach to medicine. Provides

information on how holistic health care workers treat the whole person

with an emphasis on prevention. Supports my belief that alternative

medicine can offer complementary therapies to modern medicine.

Harris, Merri. "Complementary Health Care." *Today's Health* Nov. 2008: 24-33.

Web. 14 Dec. 2008. Discusses the importance of all medical

practitioners treating the whole person. Makes a good case for why and how alternative and conventional health care practitioners should address their patients' physical, emotional, and spiritual needs. Easily accessible article with good definitions related to the "whole person" approach to medicine.

Hoey, John. "The Arrogance of Science and the Pitfalls of Hope." *Canadian Medical Association Journal* 159 (2006): 803-04. Print. Argues that when all else fails, especially with a pernicious disease such as cancer, people often seek alternative approaches to medicine. Ironically, they are driven by fear and hope to consider unconventional therapies. Hoey would like to see conventional and alternative medicine work collaboratively more often to better serve patients. He makes some strong arguments that directly support my thesis.

Micozzi, Marc. "Interview with Marc Micozzi, M.D." *Health World Online* 20 Oct. 2008: 10-14. Web. 27 Jan. 2011. Gives a clear description of his training as an M.D. which focused on treating symptoms not on prevention. Believes in individuals taking responsibility for their own health. Offers suggestions for how people can adopt a philosophy of health which would positively impact their daily lives. Good information for my conclusion.

Weil, Andrew. "Dr. Andrew Weil: Healer, Teacher, Visionary." Interview. By Parris M. Kidd. *Trio* Feb.-Mar. 2008: 18-20. Print. This interview, conducted by Paris Kidd, provides information on Dr. Andrew Weil's career in alternative medicine. He is founder, professor, and director of the Arizona Center for Integrative Medicine at the University of Arizona. He received both his medical degree and his undergraduate degree from Harvard University and established the field of integrative medicine, which aims to combine alternative and conventional medicine.

Whitaker, Julian. "Sparkling Eyes Got Me Started." *Health and Healing* 7.1 (2007): 1. Print. Defines a particular system of health that he advocates, which includes diet and herbal supplementation. He offers criticisms of modern medicine's insistence on treating symptoms only. He embraces a "system of health" like Chopra and Weil but with more of an emphasis on herbal supplementation.

SP-2 EXCERPT OF STUDENT RESEARCH PAPER IN APA FORMAT

Separate Title Page with title, name, course information, and date centered. Running head and page number ½" from top.

Traditional and Alternative: Health Care for the Future

Shanna R. Chauncey

Professor Chavez

English 103

5 January 2014

Running head is shortened version of title.

Abstract on separate page. Title and page number ½" from top as shown.

½"

1"

Abstract

This study explores the growing interest in alternative medicine and its potential as a complementary modality to conventional medicine. Although the American public still values the benefits of efficient emergency care and advanced testing procedures such as MRIs, more and more people both within the profession and without see value in the preventative approach emphasized by alternative medicine. They value alternative medicine's concern for the *health* of the whole person as it complements the highly specialized "rescue approach" to *illness* that is typical of conventional medicine. Ultimately care-givers practicing alternative medicine place the responsibility of health on the patient, which benefits both patients and the health care system.

Keywords: CAM: complementary and alternative medicine, holistic health

(excerpt) ½"

Some of the changes an alternative practitioner may suggest to a person may require sacrifice and much effort on the part of the patient. She might suggest completely transforming a patient's diet or suggest a whole different approach to exercise. These life-altering treatments return the responsibility for health to individuals. Taking responsibility for one's own health is as it should be, declares Dr. Marc Micozzi (2008), executive director of the College of Physicians of Philadelphia:

Full sentence lead-in introduces long quotation.

Use block format for quotations of more than 40 words (See section Q-3, item 2.)

Health is something that must be pursued. It's a path that people have to choose to get on. They can't be given health with a pill or an operation. It goes even beyond lifestyle. It's an issue of philosophy, and every person really has to be responsible to stay healthy, and get well when they're sick, and has to focus on their ability to care for themselves.

No page reference with this electronic source.

Commentary discussion integrates long quotation and advances the thesis.

Certainly taking such measures as reducing saturated fat or adding twenty minutes of exercise to our daily schedules constitutes positive beginning steps toward improving our well-being. But adopting a philosophy of health in daily living, as Micozzi suggests, takes time, dedication, and self-education. Such ancient systems as Chinese medicine, yoga, or Ayurvedic medicine embody whole systems of living. For example, in his book *Perfect Health*, Dr. Deepak Chopra (2013) explains that the Ayurvedic approach to health involves allowing the mind to communicate with the body at the deepest levels in order to bring first the mind then the body into balance. This is accomplished through meditation, diet, exercise, daily routines, and seasonal routines (p. 93). Other systems of health might suggest different practices for maintaining optimum health. Dr. Julian Whitaker (2007), director of Whitaker Wellness Institute, outlines the major focus of his treatments as diet, nutrition, and herbal supplementation. Like Micozzi and Chopra, he views health as a system for living. The point is that there is so much we can do in this area, so many goals worth aspiring to.

Two-sentence paraphrase with frame (lead-in and page reference). (See section S-2, guideline 3.)

Summary. No page reference with one-page article. Discussion makes clear where summary ends.

Summary. No page reference with one-page article. Discussion makes clear where summary ends.

Nobody can discount the strides modern medicine has achieved in the areas of emergency and heroic care. But now it is time to heed the cry of the masses in seeking ways to integrate mainstream and alternative medicine. Doctors such as Andrew Weil (2008) are working toward such ends. As Weil points out, the University of Arizona trains doctors to initiate programs in integrative medicine (medicine that blends conventional practices with alternative approaches) in different areas of the country. In addition, doctors in the program are learning methods in such areas as herbal medicine and mind-body medicine (p. 20). I think perhaps my father will adopt a few alternative medical therapies. He is fascinated by my vegetarian diet and makes such comments as, "Give me an example of what you would fix for dinner." On recent visits home I have caught him in the basement doing a daily stint on a treadmill. He even succumbs to regular afternoon naps, his form of relaxation or meditation.

Two-sentence summary with frame (lead-in and page reference).

Discussion integrates previous summary and advances the thesis.

Positive tone in conclusion suggests combining alternative and traditional approaches to health care.

Maybe when doctors open themselves up to practicing prevention in their own lives they will see that proof lies in experience. Elsewhere, universities and hospitals are conducting research on alternative approaches to medicine. This commitment on the part of professional health care providers can only lead to a better educated public more devoted to taking responsibility for their own health. It is a win-win situation. Doctors put an end to their fragmented rescue approach to medicine and focus on teaching people how to stay healthy. Patients concentrate on helping themselves to better health. It is only with this hand-in-hand approach that health care providers and individuals can step to a healthy rhythm into the twenty-first century.

½"

TRADITIONAL AND ALTERNATIVE   7

References on a separate page.

References

Chopra, D. (2013). *Perfect health*. New York, NY: Harmony.

Cowley, G., & Underwood, A. (2008, November 11). What's alternative? *Newsweek*, 68.

Goldberg, B. (1993). The Burton Goldberg home page. A new understanding of alternative medicine. Excerpt from *Alternative Medicine: The Definitive Guide*. Retrieved from http://www.burtongoldberg.org/altmedicine.html

Harris, M. (2008, November). Complementary health care. *Today's Health*, 24–33. Retrieved from http://www.ebsco.com

Hoey, J. (2006). The arrogance of science and the pitfalls of hope. *Canadian Medical Association Journal, 159*(9), 803–804.

Micozzi, M. (2008, October). [Interview with Daniel Redwood]. *HealthWorld Online*. Retrieved from http://www.healthy.net/library/interviews /redwood/micozzi.html

Weil, Andrew. (2008, February/March). [Interview with Parris M. Kidd]. *Trio*, 18–20.

Whitaker, J. (2007). Sparkling eyes got me started. *Health and Healing, 7*(1), 1.

SP-3 EXCERPT OF STUDENT RESEARCH PAPER IN CMS FORMAT

Separate Title Page with title, name, course information, and date centered. Running head and page number ½" from top.

Traditional and Alternative: Health Care for the Future

Shanna R. Chauncey

Professor Chavez

English 103

5 January 2014

(excerpt)   ½"

Chauncey 5

Some of the changes an alternative practitioner may suggest to a person may require sacrifice and much effort on the part of the patient. She might suggest completely transforming a patient's diet or suggest a whole different approach to exercise. These life-altering treatments return the responsibility for health to individuals. Taking responsibility for one's own health is as it should be, declares Dr. Marc Micozzi, executive director of the College of Physicians of Philadelphia:

Full-sentence lead-in introduces long quotation. Use block format for quotations of more than 40 words.

> Health is something that must be pursued. It's a path that people have to choose to get on. They can't be given health with a pill or an operation. It goes even beyond lifestyle. It's an issue of philosophy, and every person really has to be responsible to stay healthy, and get well when they're sick, and has to focus on their ability to care for themselves.[7]

Superscript ([7]) refers to endnotes.

Commentary discussion integrates long quotation and advances the thesis.

Certainly taking such measures as reducing saturated fat or adding twenty minutes of exercise to our daily schedules constitutes positive beginning steps toward improving our well-being. But adopting a philosophy of health in daily living, as Micozzi suggests, takes time, dedication, and self-education. Such ancient systems as Chinese medicine, yoga, or Ayurvedic medicine embody whole systems of living. For example, in his book *Perfect Health,* Dr. Deepak Chopra explains that the Ayurvedic approach to health involves allowing the mind to communicate with the body at the deepest levels in order to bring first the mind then the body into balance. This is accomplished through meditation, diet, exercise, daily routines, and seasonal routines.[8] Other systems of health might suggest different practices for maintaining optimum health. Dr. Julian Whitaker, director of Whitaker Wellness Institute, outlines the major focus of his treatments as diet, nutrition, and herbal supplementation.[9] Like Micozzi and Chopra, he views health as a system for living. The point is that there is so much we can do in this area, so many goals worth aspiring to.

Summary with frame (lead-in and superscript number).

Superscript ([9])

Discussion integrates previous summary and advances the thesis.

Nobody can discount the strides modern medicine has achieved in the areas of emergency and heroic care. But now it is time to heed the cry of the masses in seeking ways to integrate mainstream and alternative medicine. Doctors such as Andrew Weil are working toward such ends. As Weil points out, the University of Arizona trains doctors to initiate programs in integrative medicine (medicine that blends conventional practices with alternative approaches) in different areas of the country. In addition, doctors in the program are learning methods in such areas as herbal medicine and mind-body medicine.[10] I think perhaps my father will adopt a few alternative medical therapies. He is fascinated by my vegetarian diet and makes such comments as, "Give me an example of what you would fix for dinner." On recent visits home I have caught him in the basement doing a daily stint on a treadmill. He even succumbs to regular afternoon naps, his form of relaxation or meditation.

Superscript (^{10})

Maybe when doctors open themselves up to practicing prevention in their own lives they will see that proof lies in experience. Elsewhere, universities and hospitals are conducting research on alternative approaches to medicine. This commitment on the part of professional health care providers can only lead to a better educated public more devoted to taking responsibility for their own health. It is a win-win situation. Doctors put an end to their fragmented rescue approach to medicine and focus on teaching people how to stay healthy. Patients concentrate on helping themselves to better health. It is only with this hand-in-hand approach that health care providers and individuals can step to a healthy rhythm into the twenty-first century.

Positive tone in conclusion suggests combining alternative and traditional approaches to health care.

½"

Chauncey 7

Notes on a separate page.

Notes

1. Quoted in Cowley and Underwood, "What's Alternative?" 68.
2. Goldberg, "A New Understanding."
3. Weil, "Interview," 19.
4. Harris, "Complementary Health Care," 24.
5. Hoey, "The Arrogance of Science," 803.
6. Goldberg, "A New Understanding."
7. Micozzi, "Interview."

8. Chopra, *Perfect Health*, 93.

9. Whitaker, "Sparkling Eyes," 1.

10. Weil, "Interview," 20.

½"

Chauncey 8

Bibliography on a
separate page.

Bibliography

Chopra, Deepak. *Perfect Health*. New York: Harmony, 2013.

Cowley, Geoffrey, and Anne Underwood. "What's Alternative?" *Newsweek* November 11, 2008, 68.

The Burton Goldberg Group. *The Burton Goldberg Home Page*. Accessed February 3, 2009, http://www.burtongoldberg.org.

Harris, Merri. "Complementary Health Care." *Today's Health* November, 2008, 24–33. Accessed December 14, 2010, http://www.todayshealth/harris/complementaryhealthcare.org.

Hoey, John. "The Arrogance of Science and the Pitfalls of Hope." *Canadian Medical Association Journal* 159 (2006): 803–04.

Micozzi, Marc. "Interview with Marc Micozzi, M.D." *Health World Online* October 20, 2008: 10–14. Accessed January 27, 2011, http://healthworldonline/micozzi.

Weil, Andrew. "Dr. Andrew Weil: Healer, Teacher, Visionary." Interview. By Parris M. Kidd. *Trio,* February-March 2008, 18–20.

Whitaker, Julian. "Sparkling Eyes Got Me Started." *Health and Healing* 7, no. 1 (2007): 1.

WD-1 Living in Contemporary Society

Each generation has its own unique challenges and opportunities, and the media is quick to assign labels; the Lost Generation of the 1920s, the Beat Generation of the 1950s, the Woodstock Generation of the 1960s, the yuppies and baby boomers of the 1970s and 1980s, Generation X of the 1990s, and Generation Y or the Millennials coming of age now. Consider the generation to which you belong and try to define what makes it unique, perhaps coming up with your own label for it. What do you see as the advantages of being born when you were? Consider the attitudes, opportunities, and disadvantages you and your peers share that may not be shared by people older or younger than you, perhaps in regard to the environment, careers, money, technology, marriage, or the future.

Use the following article excerpts to write a short documented essay on life in contemporary society. By writing on this topic and documenting your essay with the sources provided, you can practice integrating and documenting source material. In a later assignment you may wish to expand your essay into a longer research paper by doing research of your own. An example of such an expanded research paper is shown in the previous section.

As with all research projects, using source material means more than merely reporting on or copying down that material. It is vital that you come to some conclusions of *your own* about the subject. Consequently, you are encouraged to read the article excerpts and then *explore your own experiences and knowledge about the topic*. Base your essay primarily on what you have experienced. Later you can pick out those ideas from the articles that explain and support your views. If you find excerpts with which you disagree, cite them and refute them in your essay by providing counterarguments. Use the source material only to support, elaborate, or disagree with *your views*. Do not allow the excerpts or your summaries of them to control your discussion. Use the **Revision Checklist** following the articles to assist you in your writing.

Documentation Requirements: You are asked to integrate information from several of the articles into your essay and include at least *one long quotation* (over four lines in MLA style or over forty words in APA style), *one short quotation*, and *one paraphrase or summary* because each has a different documentation format. Depending on the length of your essay, you will probably use more than one of each. Include a separate reference list correctly formatted in MLA, APA, or CMS. A sample research paper in the previous section shows examples of correctly formatted quotations, paraphrases, summaries, and reference lists for MLA, APA, and CMS styles. A complete list of sample reference entries is provided at the end of the book.

****

Here are some more ideas to get you started: Consider the key influences in your life, especially as they are a reflection of the times in which you grew up. How do your heroes (pop stars, movie starts, actual people) compare with the heroes of other generations? How has media and technology—MTV, Facebook, YouTube, television, music, movies, video games, I-pods, cell phones, texting, the Internet in general—shaped your attitudes and those of your generation? Examine your family life and your relationship with family members. How will your life be different from your parents? Describe the advantages and disadvantages for children whose parents both work or who come from single-parent families—a much more common phenomenon today. You may feel that you are *not* a typical member of your generation, in which case you may want to discuss how your life experiences and values differ from your peers'.

The excerpts that follow could support essays on a wide range of topics, but rather than trying to write on a scattering of topics related to your generation, narrow your focus to a few well-developed ideas *supported by your own experiences* appropriate for an essay of at least 600–800 words.

Excerpt from: *Masks and Mirrors* **by Bernard Carl Rosen, published by Praeger in Westport, Connecticut, in 2001. (195 pages)**

From page 87:

Xers yearn to be free, to be masters of their own fate. They would like to cast off the restrictions of a callous world and thumb their noses at people who have been indifferent to their needs. To the Xer freedom comes festooned with rights: the right to work or not to work at all; the right to marry or stay single, to have children or not; the right to be gay lesbian or straight.

****

Excerpts from: *Grown Up Digital: How the Net Generation Is Changing Your World* **by Don Tapscott, published by McGraw Hill in New York, in 2009. (368 pages)**

From page 75:

Our research suggests that they [Net Geners] expect to choose where and when they work; they use technology to escape traditional office space and hours; and they integrate their home and social lives with work life. Most want to be able to work in places other than an office.

From page 76:

Young people insist on freedom of choice. It is a basic feature of their media diet. Instead of listening to the top ten hits on the radio, Net Geners compose iPod playlists of thousands of songs chosen from the millions of tunes available. Interested in buying a book or a pair of shoes? Amazon offers millions of choices.

From page 77:

The search for freedom is transforming education as well. At their fingertips they have access to much of the world's knowledge. Learning for them should take place when and where they want it. So attending a lecture at a specific time and place, given by a professor in a room where they are passive recipients, seems oddly old-fashioned, if not completely inappropriate.

From page 89:

They [Net Geners] collaborate online in chat groups, play multiuser video games, use e-mail, and share files for school, work, or just for fun. They influence each other through what I call N-Fluence networks, where they discuss brands, companies, products, and services. They bring a culture of collaboration with them to work and the marketplace and are comfortable using new online tools to communicate.

From page 226:

In the 1960s, 40 percent of teens said they'd be better off without their parents. Contrast that attitude with the feelings of today's Net Geners. Roughly 80 percent of Net Geners ages 18–25 report speaking to their parents in the past day, nearly three-quarters see their parents at least once a week, and half say they see their parents daily. Nearly half call one of their parents a hero.

****

Excerpts from: *Millennials Rising: The Next Generation* by Neil Howe and William Strauss, published by Vintage Books in New York, in 2000. (415 pages)

From page 4:

As a group, Millennials are unlike any other youth generation in living memory. They are more numerous, more affluent, better educated, and more ethnically diverse. More important, they are beginning to manifest a wide array of positive social habits that older Americans no longer associate with youth, including a new focus on teamwork, achievement, modesty, and good conduct. Only a few years from now, this can-do youth revolution will overwhelm the cynics and pessimists. Over the next decade, the Millennials Generation will entirely recast the image of youth from downbeat and alienated to upbeat and engaged—with potentially seismic consequences for America.

From page 86:

Regardless of their skin color, and regardless of the diverse national origin of their parents, Millennials share the common bonds of being more wanted, protected, and cared for than the Gen Xers who preceded them. Nowhere is this better illustrated than in the great concern that parents and governments have shown toward their health, and the story of health starts from conception. Today's expectant mothers treat their *in utero* Millennials with unprecedented fuss. They take prenatal vitamins. They worry about their diet and exercise. They even worry about their worrying— and train themselves to avoid stress.

****

Excerpts from *Generation Me* by Jean M. Twenge, published by Free Press in New York, in 2007. (304 pages)

From page 5:

We [young people born in the 1970s, 1980s, and the 1990s] enjoy unprecedented freedom to pursue what makes us happy. But our expectations, combined with an increasingly competitive world, have led to a darker flip side, where we blame other people for our problems and sink into anxiety and depression. Perhaps because of the focus on the self, sexual behavior has also changed radically: these days, parents worry not just about high school sex but about junior high school sex.

From page 120:

Looked at objectively, however, things really are harder now. It was once possible to support a family on one middle-class or even working-class income. No longer. Many blue-collar jobs with good wages have been shipped overseas, and many white-collar jobs don't pay that well either.

From page 181:

GenMe may have left behind some of the good social rules about politeness, but, following in the footsteps of the Boomers, we have also left behind some of the bad social rules about everyone living life in the same way, and minorities and women staying in their 'place.' We are less likely to believe in moral absolutes, so we are tolerant and accept diversity in all its forms.

****

Excerpt from: *Rap and Hip Hop: The Voice of a Generation* by Sherry Ayazi-Hashjin, published by Rosen Publishing Group, in New York, in 1999.

From page 57:

Hip hop is a form of expression created by young people. Its roots can be traced to Africa, but it is also an art form focused on the future. It teaches us to strive for newness not only through the medium of sound but through the way we learn, create, and live our lives.

WD-2 Revision Checklist

	Yes	Needs Work
☐ Interesting Title	——	——
☐ Creative, attention-grabbing introduction	——	——
☐ Clear, public issue (thesis). Readers know how the essay relates to them	——	——
☐ Thesis repeated throughout the essay or easily inferred by readers	——	——
☐ All details and examples relate to the thesis (focus)	——	——
☐ Examples "show" rather than "tell."	——	——
☐ Sources used in paper in the form of a **summary** or **paraphrase**, **short quote**, and **long quote** (over four lines for MLA or forty words for APA)	——	——
☐ Sources are identified with lead-ins that give author's full name and some information about the author (See S-2, guideline 1)	——	——
☐ Source material is *integrated* into the text with relevant commentary before and after	——	——
☐ Summaries or paraphrases of more than one sentence are *framed* to show beginning and end (See section S-2, guideline 3)	——	——
☐ Works Cited page and documentation in correct format	——	——
☐ Eliminate major usage errors (See section WP-2)	——	——
☐ Final typed format follows sample essays (sections SP-1, SP-2, and SP-3)	——	——

WP-1 Review: Elements of the Essay

The model research papers in sections SP-1 and SP-2 identify the following elements in context.

- **Thesis:** The thesis is the central, controlling idea of the essay and is usually clearly stated early in the essay. It is what you hope your readers will gain by reading the essay; it is *their* connection to the subject, *their* reason for reading it.
- **Authentic Purpose:** Being committed to your topic and having an authentic purpose for writing is an important step in becoming an author. The authentic purpose is the reason you care about a subject and the reason you are qualified to write about it; it is *your* connection to the subject.
- **Topic Sentence:** The topic sentence is the central idea of a paragraph often stated in a sentence at the beginning.
- **Paragraph Unity:** Paragraph unity is limiting each paragraph to one central idea and staying focused on it without digressing into other related or unrelated ideas.
- **Development:** Development refers to the use of specific facts, details, explanations, and examples that support the single topic of each paragraph. Usually paragraphs of less than four sentences have not provided sufficient information to explain the topic sentence.
- **Organization:** Giving an essay a clear pattern by grouping related ideas together and ordering the ideas for maximum effect, while giving a beginning, middle, and end.
- **Focus:** An essay has a clear focus when the writer has chosen an appropriate subject, limited it properly, and stuck to it without including irrelevant information or digressions.
- **Transitions:** Transitions are words or phrases that link ideas together and create coherence in an essay. Ideally all paragraphs should begin with transitions, and transitions should also be used frequently within paragraphs to link sentences together. Transitional words: *likewise, consequently, similarly, next, finally, also, besides, actually, however, further.* Transitional phrases: *at the same time, as a result, on the other hand, in the first place, to sum up, for example, in fact, in short.*

WP-2 Review: Major Usage Errors

The quality of the content is always the most vital part of any writing. However, two things happen to the content when we fail to follow the conventions of grammar and usage: (1) the ideas become unclear or confusing, and (2) readers will not take seriously ideas that are written with obvious mechanical errors. Although grammar and usage texts can be hundreds of pages in length, students should take heart and know that there are only a few *major errors* that will seriously affect their writing. If a writer can identify and eliminate these major errors, other less serious errors will usually fall away on their own in time as a writer gains more practice.

COMMA SPLICES

The *comma splice* occurs when two independent clauses are joined, or spliced, with a comma. It is the most common type of usage error.

Incorrect: **U.S. educational policies have been almost exclusively a local concern, the federal government had virtually no presence in public education until the early 1960s.**

FUSED SENTENCES

The *fused sentence* (or run-on) is caused by incorrectly joining two independent clauses or sentences, leaving out any punctuation between them.

Incorrect: **U.S. educational policies have been almost exclusively a local concern the federal government had virtually no presence in public education until the early 1960s.**

Comma splices and fused sentences are most easily corrected by:

1. inserting a period and capital letter: . . . *a local concern. The* federal . . . .

2. inserting a coordinating conjunction (and, or, for, nor, so, yet, but): . . . *a local concern, for the federal* . . . .

3. inserting a semicolon: . . . *a local concern; the federal* . . . .

SENTENCE FRAGMENTS

A *fragment* is an incomplete sentence punctuated like a complete sentence. Because it is an incomplete thought, it will make little sense when read by itself and usually needs to be connected to the previous or following word group. Notice there is only one complete sentence in the following word groups—the others are fragments:

> **The musician's genuine talent.**
>
> **The genuinely talented musician.**
>
> **The musician playing with talent.**
>
> **For the musician to play with talent.**
>
> **Because the musician was genuinely talented.**
>
> **The musician was genuinely talented.** *(complete sentence)*

SUBJECT-VERB DISAGREEMENT

Subject-verb disagreement occurs when subjects and verbs do not agree in number. Most writers have little trouble with this error unless a sentence has several words or phrases separating the subject from the verb and it becomes unclear to the writer which word is actually the subject. If the subject is singular, the verb should be singular: *The report on automobile deaths is alarming.* If the subject is plural, the verb should be plural: *The reports on automobile deaths are alarming.*

Helpful Hints: The subject is never found in a prepositional phrase.

> *Incorrect:* **The sound of the drums are mesmerizing.** (*sound* is the subject, not *drums*)

When subjects are joined by *or, either/or, neither/ nor,* the verb agrees with the closer subject.

> **Neither the coach nor the players were** ready to accept defeat.
>
> **Neither the players nor the coach was** ready to accept defeat.

PRONOUN-ANTECEDENT DISAGREEMENT

Pronoun-antecedent disagreement occurs when pronouns do not agree in number or gender with their antecedents. Usually this error occurs because of the carryover of informal speech patterns into the more

formal situation of writing. Most pronouns substitute for other words. The following sentences have little meaning for us unless we know whom or what the underlined pronouns represent:

> **She is an exotic looking model.**
>
> **It was expensive.**
>
> **They enjoyed it.**

Because pronouns stand for other words, make sure they agree in number and gender with whatever or whomever they represent.

> **My friend bought her books at Barnes & Noble.**
>
> **My friends bought their books at Barnes & Noble.**

INDEFINITE PRONOUNS

A special problem exists when the following indefinite pronouns are used as antecedents: *anyone, anybody, each, every, everyone, everybody, everything, someone, somebody, no one, nobody.* While these are all singular, they often refer to groups composed of both genders, and thus using a singular pronoun can be misleading or sexist: *Everyone should bring his books to class.* (This would be misleading or an example of sexist language in a class composed of both men and women.) Because using the *his or her* construction often creates more problems than it solves, the use of plural pronouns to refer to these singular antecedents is becoming acceptable in speech and informal writing: *Everyone should bring their books to class.* However, in formal writing it is best to avoid the problem altogether by using plurals when possible or leaving out the pronoun.

> **All students should bring their books to class.**
>
> **Everyone should bring books to class.**

Vague "You"

The pronoun *you* represents a special problem for many student writers, again mainly because of the carryover of informal speech patterns into writing. Use *you* only when referring to a specific reader, not as a substitute for *someone.* For example, "When you get a job at McDonald's, the first thing you will do is clean the grills." Readers might wonder what you are talking about if they have no intention of working at McDonald's. Recast such sentences into either first person or third person:

First person: **When I got a job at McDonald's, the first thing I had to do was clean the grills.**

Third Person: **Those who begin working at McDonald's will find themselves cleaning the grills.**

SENTENCE STRUCTURE

Errors in *sentence structure* occur when sentences become tangled up or awkwardly worded. They may be a result of faulty comparisons, mixed constructions, misplaced modifiers, lack of parallel structure, or other problems. Identifying the exact problem is not as important as making sure your thoughts are not confusing to readers. When you suspect that you have created a sentence that readers might find hard to understand or that does not sound quite right to you, break it down into one or two short sentences. Use a conventional subject-verb-object word order, and say what you mean in clear and simple language. There will be other opportunities to write with more stylish syntax.

Sentence structure error: **By making weekly savings deposits is your best guarantee for having money for the summer.**

Simplified: **Weekly savings deposits will guarantee money for the summer.**

Sentence structure error: **The use of stream-of-consciousness in the novels of William Faulkner is as effective, if not better than Marcel Proust.**

Simplified: **William Faulkner is a better stream-of-consciousness writer than Marcel Proust.**

CLICHÉS

Clichés are predictable, overused expressions. Unfortunately, using a cliché (or figure of speech) that we have heard somewhere before will only make our writing seem stale and unoriginal, even if the expression was quite vivid at one time. Instead of using a cliché, it would be better to describe a situation in honest detail. Your writing will naturally be fresh and interesting. Avoid expressions such as the following:

seemed like an eternity	kick the habit
spread like wildfire	in this day and age
throw in the towel	crack of dawn
easier said than done	spring is in the air
crying shame	fraught with danger
quiet as a mouse	stick to your guns
walking on eggs	water off a duck's back
cold as ice	face the music
stab in the back	better late than never
draw a line in the sand	make it perfectly clear

SELF-TEST

Fill in the blank with the abbreviation of the error in each of the following sentences. Then correct the sentence as simply as possible.

CS—comma splice
FS—fused sentence/run-on
SV—subject/verb disagreement
PA—pronoun/antecedent disagreement
F—fragment
SS—sentence structure

1. Julie works as a computer programmer she translates programs into symbols that a computer reads.

1. _____

2. Each of the poems that the poet read last night were interesting.

2. _____

3. Hiking purposefully toward the ultimate goal, Mt. Rainier.

3. _____

4. Neither her pet rabbit nor her cat were upset by her long absence last summer.

4. _____

5. Although it turned into a sultry, humid day and all of us got sunburned.   5. _____

6. Many people mistakenly believe that by being wealthy is the only way to happiness.   6. _____

7. The test proved difficult, however, it was fair.   7. _____

8. Everyone should submit their homework to their instructor's e-mail address.   8. _____

9. One of the members brought their photos to the meeting while the others stored theirs for future parties.   9. _____

10. Under the new proposal, college freshmen, many of whom receive financial aid through a special grant, will be abolished.   10. _____

All answers are given for the self-tests. For the remaining exercises, only selected answers are provided. Use these to check your progress, but remember that your wording will probably differ. Headnotes indicate the degree of flexibility you may have in composing answers.

R-2 Researching a Topic

1. b	5. b	8. a
2. a, b	6. a	9. b
3. a	7. a	10. a, b, d
4. a, b		

R-3 Preparing a Bibliography and a Preliminary Thesis

1. a	6. b	11. c
2. c	7. a	12. d
3. b	8. c	13. a
4. a	9. c	14. b
5. b	10. b	15. c

R-4 Taking Notes and Outlining

1. F	6. F	11. a
2. F	7. F	12. d
3. F	8. T	13. c
4. T	9. T	14. b
5. F	10. T	15. a

Citing Sources Self-Test

1. Yes, additional citation is necessary at the end of the paragraph.

2. Common knowledge; no citation necessary.

3. Yes, citation necessary.

4. Common knowledge; no citation necessary.

5. Yes, citation required.

6. Yes, citation and quotation marks required.

7. Yes, citation required.

8. Yes, citation required.

9. Common knowledge; no citation required.

10. Yes, citation required.

11. Yes, additional citation required at the beginning of the paragraph.

12. Yes, citation required.

C-4 Practice in Recognizing Plagiarism

3. The student correctly paraphrases the author's ideas but fails to attribute them, causing the reader to think the information comes from the student writer, not authors Hall, Frayer, and Wilen. *Note:* Student revisions will vary.

4. The student uses exact wording from the original but does not set it off with quotation marks. Even borrowing short phrases verbatim without proper documentation is not acceptable and qualifies as plagiarism. *Note:* Student "revisions" will vary.

10. Student version is correctly paraphrased and documented.

C-5 Additional Practice in Recognizing Plagiarism

1. **(A)** The student paraphrases the author's ideas and attributes them correctly in the first sentence but fails to document the second sentence by providing a narrative end frame since this electronic source has no page numbers. Remember that *all* borrowed information should be documented, and the difference between the student writer's ideas and the borrowed source's ideas should be clear to the reader.

 (B) The student misrepresents the original by suggesting that the physicians actually collected the cadavers for use in anatomy schools. Changing a source's gist to fit the needs of your own paper is unacceptable.

 (C) The student uses exact wording from the original (even though it has been reordered) but does not set it off with quotation marks. *Note:* Student revisions will vary.

S-4 Practice in Documenting Summaries

The following answers show the correct form and placement of documentation, but student summary statements will vary.

1. *MLA:* **Genetic research is making it possible for parents to choose the sex of their child (Lemonick 64).**

 APA: **Genetic research is making it possible for parents to choose the sex of their child (Lemonick, 2013, p. 64).**

3. *MLA:* Abortion, gun control, homosexuality—most all political issues, declares Professor of Political Science David Boaz, can be reduced to debates about basic rights (par. 6).

   APA: Abortion, gun control, homosexuality—most all political issues, declares Professor of Political Science Boaz (2008), can be reduced to debates about basic rights (para. 6).

5. *MLA:* The encyclopedia entry "Rhythm and Blues" defines rhythm and blues as a type of black popular music heavily influenced by blues and gospel. It originated in the 1940s and became known as soul music in the 1960s and 1970s. The entry titled "Rhythm and Blues" states that because of its defined rhythms, this music inspires singing groups and dancers.

   APA: The 2007 encyclopedia entry "Rhythm and Blues" defines rhythm and blues . . . . The article suggests . . . inspires singing groups and dancers.

S-5 Practice in Writing and Documenting Summaries

The following answers show the correct form and placement of documentation, but student summary statements will vary.

5. *MLA:* In her book *Mother Teresa: Beyond the Image,* Anne Selba points out that belief systems provide much-needed support in a technologically advanced society (195).

   APA: In her book *Mother Teresa: Beyond the Image,* A. Selba (2007) points out that . . . advanced society (p. 195).

7. *MLA:* Author Anne Meyer, director of the Schools Without Drugs Council, advises parents and teachers to educate children about the detrimental consequences of drug use through their actions and words (115).

   APA: A. Meyer (2009), director of the . . . through their actions and words (p. 115).

10. *MLA:* Journalist Kay McElrath Johnson states that while by some appearances Kimarie Hanson typified a normal adolescent, at the age of eighteen she was the youngest woman to ever finish the Iditarod.

    APA: Journalist Kay McElrath Johnson (2009) states . . . ever finish the Iditarod.

P-4 Practice in Documenting Paraphrases

The following answers show the correct form and placement of documentation, but student paraphrases will vary.

2. (a) *MLA:* Walter Isaacson, senior staff writer for *Time*, notes that our DNA has changed by only 2% since humans have gone on a separate path from the apes five million years ago (43).

   APA: Isaacson (2013), senior staff writer for *Time*, notes that . . . (p. 43).

   (b) *MLA:* Our DNA has changed by only 2% since humans have gone on a separate path from the apes five million years ago (Isaacson 43).

   APA: Our DNA has changed . . . five million years ago (Isaacson, 2013, p. 43).

4. (a) *MLA:* Society supports the "model look" for female athletes when they're not participating in their sport, believes former Olympic women's basketball player, Jesse Sherwood, but we turn around and expect them to don the athletic build when they are participating in sports.

   APA: Society supports . . . believes former Olympic women's basketball player, Jesse Sherwood (2008), but we turn . . . in sports.

   (b) *MLA:* Society supports the "model look" for female athletes when they're off the field or court, but we turn around and expect them to don the athletic build when they are participating in sports believes former Olympic women's basketball player Jesse Sherwood.

   APA: Society supports the "model look" . . . believes former Olympic women's basketball player Sherwood (2008).

84

P-5 Practice in Writing and Documenting Paraphrases

The following answers show the correct form and placement of documentation, but student paraphrases will vary.

2. **MLA:** We control and dominate the natural environment by developing it in the face of our recent knowledge that all life is interrelated (Thomas 102).

   APA: We control and dominate the natural environment . . . is interrelated (Thomas, 2012, p. 102).

3. **MLA:** Jared Diamond notes that researchers have discovered that in the past 50,000 years when humans have arrived at a certain destination, a major extinction has followed (23).

   APA: Diamond (2002) notes that researchers . . . has followed (p. 23).

7. **MLA:** Maintaining a livable environment may involve individuals sacrificing certain valued commodities (Stewart).

   APA: Maintaining a livable . . . (Stewart, 2008).

P-6 Additional Practice in Writing and Documenting Paraphrases

The following answers show the correct form and placement of documentation, but student paraphrases will vary.

1. **MLA:** James Cappella, a sociologist who researches dreams, states in his book *Dream Studies* that men and woman differ in what they dream about, and in our lifetimes humans spend a total of approximately six full years dreaming (43).

   Note: For MLA it is necessary to cite both the author and the title of the work since two works by the same author are being used.

   APA: Cappella (2007), a sociologist who researches dreams . . . six full years dreaming (p. 43).

3. **MLA:** Aristotle believed that dream content is affected by personal feelings since we do not rely on our senses while we are asleep ("Diverse Views").

APA: Aristotle believed that dreams . . . rely on our senses while we are asleep ("Diverse Views," 2013).

6. **MLA:** While the background details and people may not remain identical, Paul Dokes, a psychiatrist specializing in dream analysis, explains that dreams will often repeat similar themes, which tend to be more negative than positive (54).

   APA: While the background details and people may not remain identical, Dokes (2012), a psychiatrist . . . more negative than positive (p. 54).

Q-4 Practice in Punctuating Quotations

The following answers show the correct form, placement, and punctuation of the documentation. Student answers should *not* vary.

1. **MLA:** "Can you hoodwink time and retard the aging process?" ask Bechtel and Waggoner (127).

   APA: "Can you hoodwink time and retard the aging process?" ask Bechtel and Waggoner (2012, p. 127).

6. **MLA:** "The disappearance of drive-in movie theaters represents the loss of a significant part of American culture," observes movie critic Pat Sondheim (qtd. in Disch 94).

   APA: "The disappearance of drive-in movie theaters represents the loss of a significant part of American culture," observes movie critic Pat Sondheim (cited in Disch, 2013, p. 94).

3. **MLA:** In William Shakespeare's sonnet "That Time of Year Thou Mayst in Me Behold" the speaker compares his own aging process to the end of a day:

   > In me thou see'st the twilight of such day
   > As after sunset fadeth in the west,
   > Which by-and-by black night doth take away,
   > Death's second self that seals up all in rest. (lines 5-8)

APA: In William Shakespeare's (1609) sonnet "That Time of Year Thou Mayst in Me Behold" the speaker compares his own aging process to the end of a day:

> In me thou see'st the twilight of such day
>
> As after sunset fadeth in the west,
>
> Which by-and-by black night doth take away,
>
> Death's second self that seals up all in rest. (lines 5–8)

Q-5 Additional Practice in Punctuating Quotations

The following answers show the correct form, placement, and punctuation of the documentation. Student answers should *not* vary.

1. **MLA:** Monroe asks, "Is deregulation enough to eliminate the years of subsidies oil and natural gas have received?" (21).

   APA: Monroe (2013) asks, "Is deregulation enough to eliminate the years of subsidies oil and natural gas have received?" (p. 21).

3. **MLA:** The legends and myths of the Pueblo Indians are "enmeshed in the web of the universe" and pulsate with both animate and inanimate life forms (Erdoes 11).

   APA: The legends and myths of the Pueblo Indians are "enmeshed in the web of the universe" and pulsate with both animate and inanimate life forms (Erdoes, 2013, p. 11).

7. **MLA:** Van Dyk, author of the book *In Afghanistan,* states, "One of the world's great rivers, the Brahmaputra, begins as a glacial trickle in western Tibet and sweeps 1,800 miles to the Indian Ocean" (372).

   APA: Van Dyk (2012), author of the book *In Afghanistan,* states, "One of the world's great rivers, the Brahmaputra, begins as a glacial trickle in western Tibet and sweeps 1,800 miles to the Indian Ocean" (p. 372).

Q-6 Practice in Creating Lead-Ins for Quotations

The following answers show the correct form and placement of lead-ins and documentation. Wording of the lead-ins may vary.

4. **MLA:** Photography seminar leaders Tim Davis and Renee Lynn agree, "Usually when the sun casts a warm glow in the early morning hours or toward the end of day, the light wraps around and flatters the subject" (46).

   "Usually when the sun casts a warm glow in the early morning hours or toward the end of day," photography seminar leaders Tim Davis and Renee Lynn contend, "the light wraps around and flatters the subject" (46).

   "Usually when the sun casts a warm glow in the early morning hours or toward the end of day, the light wraps around and flatters the subject," comment photography seminar leaders Tim Davis and Renee Lynn (46).

   APA: Photography seminar leaders Tim Davis and Renee Lynn (2013) agree, "Usually when the sun casts a warm glow in the early morning hours or toward the end of day, the light wraps around and flatters the subject" (p. 46).

   "Usually when the sun casts a warm glow in the early morning hours or toward the end of day," photography seminar leaders Tim Davis and Renee Lynn contend, "the light wraps around and flatters the subject" (2013, p. 46).

   "Usually when the sun casts a warm glow in the early morning hours or toward the end of day, the light wraps around and flatters the subject," comment photography seminar leaders Tim Davis and Renee Lynn (2013, p. 46).

5. **MLA:** Olympic trainer Tanya Sommerfield grants, "Adopting a positive habit like exercise can be as tough as breaking a bad one like smoking" (qtd. in Krocoff). *Note:* Online source. No page reference available.

"Adopting a positive habit like exercise," emphasizes Olympic trainer Tanya Sommerfield, "can be as tough as breaking a bad one like smoking" (qtd. in Krocoff).

"Adopting a positive habit like exercise can be as tough as breaking a bad one like smoking," observes Olympic trainer Tanya Sommerfield (qtd. in Krocoff).

APA: Olympic trainer Tanya Sommerfield grants, "Adopting a positive habit like exercise can be as tough as breaking a bad one like smoking" (cited in Krocoff, 2009).

"Adopting a positive habit like exercise," emphasizes Olympic trainer Tanya Sommerfield, "can be as tough as breaking a bad one like smoking" (cited in Krocoff, 2009).

"Adopting a positive habit like exercise can be as tough as breaking a bad one like smoking," observes Olympic trainer Tanya Sommerfield (cited in Krocoff, 2009).

Q-7 Practice in Integrating, Punctuating, and Documenting Quotations

The following answers show the correct form and placement of documentation. Wording of the lead-ins may vary.

3. *MLA:* "Though Italians were frequently depicted as criminals, they were also often seen as comically hot-tempered waiters, barbers, or musicians," notes movie critic Roger Dooley.

APA: "Though Italians were frequently depicted as criminals, they were also often seen as comically hot-tempered waiters, barbers, or musicians," notes movie critic Roger Dooley (2013).

4. *MLA:* Police chief Jerry Galvin states, "Why Albuquerque, a city of 400,000, would need a full-time paramilitary unit is a question that should have been asked years ago" (qtd. in Egan 16).

APA: Police chief Jerry Galvin states, "Why Albuquerque, a city of 400,000, would need a full-time paramilitary unit is a question that should have been asked years ago" (cited in Egan, 2013, p. A16).

Q-8 Additional Practice in Integrating, Punctuating, and Documenting Quotations

The following answers show the correct form and placement of documentation. Wording of the lead-ins may vary.

2. *MLA:* "The show *Jeopardy!* never forces contestants to discover the 'why' of a question," notes entertainment editor Franz Lidz. "Therefore, it can be said that the show is both a cause and a symptom of the Information Age's lust for naked data" (94).

APA: "The show *Jeopardy!* never forces contestants to discover the 'why' of a question," notes entertainment editor F. Lidz (2007). "Therefore, it can be said that the show is both a cause and a symptom of the Information Age's lust for naked data" (p. 94).

3. *MLA:* "How many people know that Bette Midler dealt with poverty and racism when she was one of the few white kids in her Hawaiian school?" asks Clea Simon, staff writer for the *Boston Globe.*

APA: "How many people know that Bette Midler dealt with poverty and racism when she was one of the few white kids in her Hawaiian school?" asks Clea Simon, staff-writer for the *Boston Globe* (2008).

Q-9 Common Errors in Citing Sources (Self Test)

1. Donald Grey asks, "Is there any solution to the devastation global warming will cause?" (34).

   Errors: Rule 1. Avoid redundancy in citation and incorrect placement of quotation marks.

2. In the book *Romance Is Illusion* by Carl Zimmer it states, "Love is pure magic" (120).

   Errors: Rule 3. Avoid wordiness and redundancy in lead-ins and incorrect placement of period.

3. "Voters sense that politics is an act," asserts Klein (72).

   Errors: Rule 6 and Rule 7. All direct quotes require narrative lead-ins and parenthetical citation must follow style format exactly including only the information prescribed by the format.

4. Barack Obama explains, "I am the son of a man from Kenya and a woman from Kansas" (qtd. in Barnes).

   Error: Rule 5. When you quote or paraphrase material that is being quoted by someone else, use *qtd. in* (MLA) or *cited in* (APA) to clarify the source.

5. Mark Tolson declares, "We live in techno-enthusiastic times."

   Errors: Rule 4. Do not use *quotes* as a verb in lead-ins. Also set off lead-ins with commas and capitalize the first word of a quoted sentence.

W-4 Practice in Punctuating MLA Works Cited

Alexander, Jenni. "Batik on Film." Journal of Visual Arts 3 (2008): 122-34. Web. 1 June 2008.

"An Analysis of Worker Drug Use and Workplace Policies and Programs." National Opinion Research Center. 20 July 2013. Web. 7 Sept. 2013.

Atwan, Robert. Foreword. The Best American Essays. By Elizabeth Hardwick. New York: Ticknor, 2006. 9-15. Print.

Brown, Serjom. International Relations in a Changing Global System. New York: Westview, 2013. Print.

W-5 Practice in Punctuating APA References

Alexander, J. (2008). Batik on film. Journal of Visual Arts, *3*, 122–134. Retrieved from http://www.cultronixjourn .edu/o1alex.

Atwan, R. (2006). Foreword. In E. Hardwick, The best American essays (pp. 9–15). New York, NY: Ticknor.

Brown, S. (2013). International relations in a changing global system. New York, NY: Westview.

Eiler, J., Wathen, W. G., & Pelton, M. R. (2006, April). Reproduction in black bears in the southern Appalachian mountains. Journal of Wildlife Management, *53*(2), 353–360.

Usage Errors Self-Test

1. FS	6. SS
2. SV	7. CS
3. F	8. PA
4. SV	9. PA
5. F	10. SS

The *Chicago Manual of Style* (CMS) uses two basic documentation systems: (1) notes and bibliography and (2) author-date. In the author-date system sources are cited in the text, usually in parentheses, by author's last name, date of publication and page: (Ward and Burns 2011, 35). This system is similar to the American Psychological Association style (APA) used throughout this book. The notes and bibliography system uses superscript numbers[1] in the text of the paper that correspond to numbers in footnotes or endnotes. Numbers are cited sequentially and each number has a corresponding note. If all of the publication information is included in the notes, it is not necessary to have a separate Bibliography list. It is recommended that students include a separate Bibliography and then use an abbreviated format for the notes. The following models show the correct format for a complete note, an abbreviated note, and a Bibliography entry. CMS allows articles in newspapers, magazines, reference works, blogs, and e-mails to be cited in the narrative lead-in without subsequent reference in notes or bibliography. The following examples show the more formal versions of all citations and are based on the *Chicago Manual of Style*, 16th edition, web site cited above.

A Book by One Author

1. Henry Scott Stokes, *The Life and Death of Yukio Mishima* (New York: Noonday, 2013), 73.
2. Stokes, *The Life and Times*, 73.
Stokes, Henry Scott. *The Life and Death of Yukio Mishima.* New York: Noonday, 2013.

A Book by Two or Three Authors

1. John E. Engelmayer, Jerome Davidson, and Robert M. Wagman, *Lord's Justice* (Garden City, NY: Anchor, 2008), 122.
2. Englemayer, Davidson, and Wagman, *Lord's Justice*, 122.
Engelmayer, John E., Jerome Davidson, and Robert M. Wagman. *Lord's Justice*. Garden City, NY: Anchor, 2008.

A Book by Four or More Authors

1. Thomas Kendall et al. *The Amber Wars and the Development of Europe*. (New York: Shirlington, 2007), 102.
2. Kendall et al., *Amber Wars*, 102.
Kendall, Thomas, William Reville, Seymour Hersh, and Stacey Burling. *The Amber Wars and the Development of Europe*. New York: Shirlington, 2007.

A Book with One or More Editors

1. Catherine Belsey and Jane Moore, eds., *The Feminist Reader: Essays in Gender and the Politics of Literary Criticsm* (London: Macmillan, 2009), 25–26.
2. Catherine Belsey and Jane Moore, *Feminist Reader*, 23–24.
Belsey, Catherine, and Jane Moore, eds. *The Feminist Reader: Essays in Gender and the Politics of Literary Criticsm*. London: Macmillan, 2009.

A Work in an Anthology

1. Annie Dillard, "Hidden Pennies," *Essays for Explication*, ed. Charles Wheeler (New York: Holt, 2009), 278.
2. Dillard, "Hidden Pennies," 278.
Dillard, Annie. "Hidden Pennies." *Essays for Explication*, ed. Charles Wheeler. New York: Holt, 2009.

Article in a Print Journal (If no author is identified begin with the title.)

1. Jeffrey Magee, "Revisiting Style and Form in 'Copenhagen,'" *Journal of American Musicological Society* 68, no. 5 (2004): 490.
2. Magee, "Revisiting Style," 490.

Magee, Jeffrey. "Revisiting Style and Form in 'Copenhagen.'" *Journal of American Musicological Society* 68, no. 5 (2004): 485–494.

Article in a Newspaper or Popular Magazine (If no author is identified begin with the title.)

1. Daniel Mendelsohn, "Winds of Change," *New Yorker*, January 29, 2011, 32.
2. Mendelsohn, "Winds," 32.
Mendelsohn, Daniel. "Winds of Change." *New Yorker*, January 29, 2011, 30–32.
1. "The Power of Ideas," *St. Louis Post-Dispatch*, February 14, 2011, B14.
2. "The Power of Ideas," B14.
"The Power of Ideas." *St. Louis Post-Dispatch*, February 14, 2011, B14.

A Government Document

1. Central Intelligence Agency, *The World Fact Book 2011* (Washington, DC: Potomac Books, 2011), 170.
2. Central Intelligence Agency, *World Fact*, 170.
Central Intelligence Agency, *The World Fact Book 2011*. Washington, DC: Potomac Books, 2011.

A Video or Recording

1. *The Last Picture Show*, directed by Peter Bogdanovich (1976; Burbank, CA: RCA/Columbia Pictures Home Video, 2005), DVD.
2. *The Last Picture Show*.
The Last Picture Show. Directed by Peter Bogdanovich. 1976; Burbank, CA: RCA/Columbia Pictures Home Video, 2005. DVD.

ELECTRONIC SOURCES

Journal Article from Database

Include a DOI (Digital Object Identifier) if the journal lists one. The DOI when appended to http://dx.doi.org/ will lead to the source. If no DOI is available, list a URL. Include an access date only if required by your instructor.

1. Merlin Wynne, "The Course of Irish History," *American Journal of Sociology* 119 (2011): 322, *EBSCOhost*, accessed February 17, 2011, doi:10.1086/599245.

2. Wynne, "Irish History," 322.

Wynne, Merlin. "The Course of Irish History." *American Journal of Sociology* 119 (2011): 320–34. *EBSCOhost.* Accessed February 17, 2011. doi:10.1086/599245.

Article from Sponsoring Organization

1. "McDonald's Nutrition Facts," McDonald's Corporation, accessed March 12, 2011, http://www.mcdonalds.com/corp/about/factssheet.html.

2. "McDonald's Nutrition."

McDonald's Corporation. "McDonald's Nutrition Facts." Accessed March 12, 2011. http://www.mcdonalds.com/corp/about/factssheet.html.

Wiki

1. "Chimpanzees," Wikipedia, accessed March 2, 2011, http://www.chimpanzees.com/ wiki/wikipedia-found.

2. "Chimpanzees."

Wikipedia. "Chimpanzees." Accessed March 2, 2011, http://www.chimpanzees.com/wiki/wikipedia-found.

Blog

1. Sandra Brock, February 26, 2011 (4:48 p.m.), comment on Phyllis Fuentes, "Ozone and Our Future," *Seattle Times Blog,* February 21, 2011, http://SeattleTimes.com_21feb11//ozone.

2. Brock, comment on Fuentes, "Ozone."

Seattle Times Blog. http://SeattleTimes.com_21feb11//ozone.

REFERENCES

Books

A Book by One Author

Stokes, H. S. (2004). *The life and death of Yukio Mishima.* New York, NY: Noonday.

Two or More Books by the Same Author

MacLaine, S. (2005). *It's all in the playing.* Toronto, Ontario: Bantam.

MacLaine, S. (2007). *My lucky stars.* New York, NY: Bantam.

A Book by Two or Three Authors

Engelmayer, J. E., Davidson, J., & Wagman, R. M. (2008). *Lord's justice.* Garden City, NY: Anchor.

A Book by Four or More Authors

Kendall, T., Sutherland, W., Feinstein, R., & Randolph, E. (2007). *The amber wars and the development of Europe.* New York, NY: Shirlington.

A Book with One or More Editors

Belsey, C., & Moore, J. (Eds.). (2006). *The feminist reader: Essays in gender and the politics of literary criticism.* London, England: Macmillan.

A Work in an Anthology

Dillard, A. (2004). Hidden pennies. In C. Wheeler (Ed.), *Essays for explication* (pp. 110–111). New York, NY: Holt.

An Introduction, Preface, Foreword, or Afterword

Scanlan, L. (2001). Introduction. In M. Roberts, *The man who listens to horses* (pp. xiii–xlii). New York, NY: Random.

An Illustrated Book or Graphic Novel

Moore, Alan. (1987). *Swamp thing.* Illus. Dave Gibbons. New York, NY: Warner Books.

Articles

Article in a Scholarly Journal (include volume and issue number)

Magee, J. (2004). Revisiting style and form in "Copenhagen." *Journal of American Musicological Society, 68*(5), 42–66.

An Article in a Monthly or Bimonthly Magazine

Schuster, A. M. H. (2003, July/August). Colorful cotton. *Archaeology, 48,* 40–45.

An Article in a Weekly or Biweekly Magazine

Taylor, C. (2004, January 18). The history and the hype. *Time, 153,* 72–73.

A Signed Article in a Newspaper

Vogel, S. (2008, February 9). Marines fault pilot for alpine accident. *The Washington Post,* p. A3.

An Unsigned Article in a Newspaper

Toymaker has plans for Barbie at 40: A hip look, including a tattoo. (1999, February 4). *St. Louis Post-Dispatch,* p. A2.

An Editorial in a Newspaper

Employers can limit free speech. (2007, February 5). *San Francisco Chronicle,* p. 21.

A Government Document

OECD Council. (2007). *Improving ethical conduct in the public service.* Washington DC: U.S. Government Printing Office.

Oregon State. (2007). Commission for Technological Safety. *Creating safe work environments in a technological age.* Portland, OR: State of Oregon.

An Interview

Fields, R. (2008, April). In light of death [Interview with Helen Tworkov]. *The Sun,* 10–14.

A Reference Work

Standen, E. (2004). Lace. , *The encyclopedia Americana* (Vol. 16, p. 106). Danbury, CT: Grolier.

An Unsigned Article in a Reference Work

Poisons and poisoning. (2003). *The encyclopaedia Britannica* (Vol. 8, p. 586). Chicago: Encyclopaedia Britannica.

A Book or a Pamphlet by Corporate Authors

School of Public Affairs. (2004). *Report from the Institute for Philosophy and Public Policy.* Baltimore, MD: University of Maryland Press.

A Film or a Recording

Goldwyn, S. (Producer), & Hawks, H. (Director). (1941). *Ball of fire* [Film]. Hollywood, CA: MGM.

The Beatles. (1967). Lucy in the sky with diamonds. On *Sgt. Pepper's Lonely Hearts Club Band* [record]. Hollywood: Apple Records.

A Television or Radio Program

York, J. (Producer). (2001, July 26). *CNN crossfire.* New York, NY: CNN.

Lexington, M. (Producer). (2004, October 10). The bottom line. In *All things considered.* National Public Radio. Jacksonville, FL: WJCT.

NOTE: All cited sources, whether print or electronic, should have enough information so that a reader can locate them. Unless you are citing a work that is likely to change or be updated, it is not necessary to include the date you access it. However, if the most recent change or update is not clear from the entry, put *(n.d.)* in place of the date and include the retrieval date. If available, use a DOI (Digital Object Identifier) in place of a URL. DOI numbers are being used on some scholarly journals in the sciences and social sciences. For a complete list of all types of electronic sources, check the APA web site listed above. The APA makes line breaks *before* slashes and punctuation in URLs or DOIs.

DATABASES

Article from Database
Wynne, M. (2013). The times were changing. *Psychology Today, 32*(7), 23–31. doi:10.1207/s14478974psy2988_6

Kidd, P. (n.d.). Alcohol and aging. *HealthWorld* 72–76. Retrieved March 2, 2013, from <http://www.healthy.net/library/interviews/redwood/micozzi.html>

INTERNET SITES
The basic information needed to cite electronic sources is:
Name of the author (if given)
Date of publication or update; date of retrieval is required only if you think the source might change or if no publication date is available.
Document title, description, and/or source
URL or DOI (if given)

Wiki
Chimpanzees. (n.d.). *Wikipedia*. Retrieved January 14, 2011, from http://www.chimpanzees.com/wiki/Wikipedia_Found

Blog
Fuentes, P. (2008, 16 May). Ozone and our future. *The Seattle Times*. Message posted to http://SeattleTimes.com_16may08//ozone

Podcast
Bungee jumping. (2011, June 17). *BBC World Service*. Retrieved from http://www.hbes.com/HCCS/200

Online Audio or Video
Washington Forum. (2011, June 2). Barack Obama. *YouTube*. Retrieved from http://www.youtube/stat.fle.obama/

Article from Sponsoring Organization
World Conservation Monitoring Center. (2011, May 7). Wildlife at risk. Retrieved from http://Defenders.org/atrisk

Scholarly Journal from Google Scholar (or other search engine)
Press, W. (2005). Early childhood education. *Journal of Communication, 45*(1). Retrieved from http://www.stat.fle.educ/comm/journals/earl.html

Stapleton, S. (2010). Alternative medicine: Time to talk. *American Medical News, 41*(5). doi:22220.2738/c2998372amer3309_3

Periodical/Magazine
Burness, H. (2005, November 17). Economic forecast is positive. *National Business Employment Weekly*. Retrieved from http://www.business.com/economics/article.ret/html

Newspaper
Glazier, L. (2013, April 15). Arbitrary values and contemporary music. *New York Times on the Web*. Retrieved from http//www.nytimes.com/AP-/values/html

Online Book
Brown, M. (2011). *The world fact book*. Washington, DC: GPO. Retrieved from http://www.odci.gov/cia/publications/factbook/index.html

Article in a Reference Database
Douglas fir. (2011). In *Britannica Online* (Vol. 15, pp. 354–57). Retrieved from http://www.eb.com:240

Online Posting
Monaghan, P. (2009, March 4). Psychology and law. Retrieved from http://news:comp.edu.psychol

Online Scholarly Project
Mohs, J. P. (Ed.). (2008, April). *Empowering students project*. University of Chicago Writing Program. Retrieved from http://www.chicago.edu/-engdept/html/

Synchronous Communication [MUD (multiuser domain) or MOO (multiuser domain, object oriented)]
Stickney, M. (2007, December 12). It's a free day: A comparison of long-term substitute teaching in two inner city high school classrooms. Retrieved from telnet://lingua.uocolum.edu.9090

Government Document
Census Bureau. (2009, February 3). *Income 1947–2007 chartbook*. Retrieved from http://www.census.gov/hhes/income/chartbk.html

SAMPLE MLA ENTRIES

WORKS CITED

Books

A Book by One Author
Stokes, Henry Scott. *The Life and Death of Yukio Mishima*. New York: Noonday, 2004. Print.

Two or More Books by the Same Author
MacLaine, Shirley. *It's All in the Playing*. Toronto: Bantam, 2005. Print.
---. *My Lucky Stars*. New York: Bantam, 2007. Print.

A Book by Two or Three Authors
Engelmayer, John E., Jerome Davidson, and Robert M. Wagman. *Lord's Justice*. Garden City, Anchor, 2008. Print.

A Book by Four or More Authors
Kendall, Thomas, et al. *The Amber Wars and the Development of Europe*. New York: Shirlington, 2007. Print.

A Book with One or More Editors
Belsey, Catherine, and Jane Moore, eds. *The Feminist Reader: Essays in Gender and the Politics of Literary Criticism*. London: Macmillan, 2006. Print.

A Work in an Anthology
Dillard, Annie. "Hidden Pennies." *Essays for Explication*. Ed. Charles Wheeler. New York: Holt, 2004. 110-11. Print.

An Introduction, Preface, Foreword, or Afterword
Scanlan, Lawrence. Introduction. *The Man Who Listens to Horses*. By Monty Roberts. New York: Random, 2001. xiii-xlii. Print.

An Illustrated Book or Graphic Novel
Moore, Alan. *Swamp Thing*. Illus. Dave Gibbons. New York: Warner Books, 1987. Print.

Articles

Article in a Scholarly Journal (include volume and issue number)
Magee, Jeffrey. "Revisiting Style and Form in 'Copenhagen.'" *Journal of American Musicological Society* 68.5 (2004): 42-66. Print.

An Article in a Monthly or Bimonthly Magazine
Schuster, Angela M. H. "Colorful Cotton." *Archaeology* July-Aug. 2010: 40-45. Print.

An Article in a Weekly or Biweekly Magazine
Taylor, Chris. "The History and the Hype." *Time* 18 Jan. 2011: 72-73. Print.

A Signed Article in a Newspaper
Vogel, Steve. "Marines Fault Pilot for Alpine Accident." *Washington Post* 9 Feb. 2011: A3. Print.

An Unsigned Article in a Newspaper
"Toymaker Has Plans for Barbie at 40: A Hip Look, Including a Tattoo." *St. Louis Post-Dispatch* 4 Feb. 2009: A2. Print.

An Editorial in a Newspaper
"Employers Can Limit Free Speech." Editorial. *San Francisco Chronicle* 5 Feb. 2010: 21. Print.

A Government Document
United States. OECD Council. *Ethical Conduct in the Public Service*. Washington: GPO, 2007. Print.
Oregon State. Commission for Technological Safety. *Creating Safe Work Environments in a Technological Age*. Portland: State of Oregon, 2009. Print.

An Interview
Fields, Rick. "In Light of Death." Interview. By Helen Tworkov. *The Sun* Apr. 2014: 10-14. Print.

A Reference Work
Standen, Edith. "Lace." *The Encyclopedia Americana*. 2010 ed. Print.

An Unsigned Article in a Reference Work
"Poisons and Poisoning." *The Encyclopaedia Britannica*. 15th ed. 2011. Print.

A Book or a Pamphlet by Corporate Authors
School of Public Affairs. *Report from the Institute for Philosophy and Public Policy*. Baltimore: U of Maryland P, 2004. Print.

Additional Common Sources

A Film or a Recording
Ball of Fire. Dir. Howard Hawks. Perf. Gary Cooper and Barbara Stanwyck. MGM, 1941. Film.
The Beatles. "Lucy in the Sky with Diamonds." *Sgt. Pepper's Lonely Hearts Club Band*. Apple Records, 1967. LP.

A Television or Radio Program
"Need More Vacation?" *CNN Crossfire*. Narr. Mike Kinsley and Fred Smith. CNN. 26 July 2001. Television.
Douglas, Kirk. Interview by Terry Gross. *Fresh Air*. NPR. WHYY, Philiadelphia, 20 June 2008. Radio.

Personal Interview
Jones, Tanya. Personal interview. 9 June 2008.

NOTE: All cited sources, whether print or electronic, should have enough information so that a reader can locate them. MLA recognizes that sometimes it is necessary to improvise with whatever information is available. Because electronic pages can change or disappear, MLA includes the date you accessed the site in addition to the publication date. If no update or publication date is available use the abbreviation *n.d.* To ensure that you are using the latest guidelines, you may want to check the web site above.

DATABASES

The Internet can provide fast, accessible information, but most academic research should be based primarily on articles that have been published in reputable print periodicals. These are available electronically through databases at most libraries. Since these sources usually have print equivalents, give information in the appropriate print format and then add the information about the electronic source: name of database (italicized), medium of publication (Web), and date of access.

Article from a Library Subscription Database

Miller, Thomas R. "Interview with Marc Micozzi." *HealthWorld.* 19.5 (2012): 17-20. *EBSCOhost.* Web. 27 Jan. 2014.

Stapleton, Stephanie. "Alternative Medicine: Time to Talk." *American Medical News* 14 Dec. 2008: 26-27. *ProQuest.* Web. 22 Jan. 2014.

Scholarly Journal from Google Scholar (or other search engine)

Press, William. "Early Childhood Education." *Journal of Communication* 45.1 (2005). *Google Scholar.* Web. 7 Feb. 2014.

INTERNET SITES

Most general Internet sites will require the following information:
   Author, director, editor, narrator, performer, or translator
   Title of work or article
   Title of periodical or overall web site (italicized) if distinct from title of work
   Sponsor or publisher of the site
   Date last updated or publication date (if unavailable, use n.d.)
   Medium of publication (Web)
   Date accessed

Wiki

"Chimpanzees." *Wikipedia.* Wikipedia Foundation, 2011. Web. 12 July 2013.

Blog

Fuentes, Phyllis. "Ozone and Our Future." *Seattle Times.* SeattleTimes.com, 16 May 2008. Web. 13 July 2013.

Podcast

"Bungee Jumping." *BBC World Service.* BBC, 17 June 2010. Web. 8 Jan. 2014.

Online Audio or Video

Washington Forum. "Barack Obama." *YouTube.* YouTube, 12 June 2008. Web. 11 Jan. 2014.

Article by Sponsoring Organization (no author)

"Wildlife at Risk." *World Conservation Monitoring Center.* 20 June 2001. Web. 12 Dec. 2013.

Article in Periodical/Magazine

Burness, Howard. "Economic Forecast Is Positive." *National Business Employment Weekly Online* 15 Nov. 2006. Web. 17 Nov. 2013.

Newspaper Article

Glazier, Lawrence. "Arbitrary Values and Contemporary Music." *New York Times on the Web* 15 Apr. 2013. Web. 18 Aug. 2013.

Online Scholarly Project

Moser, John P., ed. *Empowering Students.* U of Chicago Writing Program, n.d. Web. 12 Sept. 2013.

Online Professional or Personal Site

Walker, James. Home page. 4 May 2008. Web. 10 Aug. 2013.

Online Posting

Richards, Jeremy. Online posting. "David Jones." Home page. By Jones. *MySpace.com.* N.p. 14 July 2011. Web. 19 July 2013.

Online Book

Brown, Marcus. *The World Factbook.* Washington: GPO, 2008. Web. 1 Sept. 2013.

Article in a Reference Database

"Douglas Fir." *Britannica Online.* Vers. 13.1. Encyclopedia Britannica. 2013. Web. 21 Oct. 2013.

Government Document

United States. Census Bureau. *Income 1947-1997 Chartbook.* 3 Feb. 2006. Web. 12 Mar. 2013.

E-mail Communication

Simpson, Steve. "Euthanasia Report." Message to Tom Moore. 3 Mar. 2014. E-mail.

Publications on CD-ROM in MLA

Note: Works on diskette or magnetic tape are also formatted as below. Indicate publication medium (CD-ROM, diskette, magnetic tape).

Scholarly Journal

Press, Willima. "Early Childhood Education." *Journal of Communication* 45.1 (2005): 10-25. *Magazine Index Plus.* CD-ROM.

Newspaper

Glazier, Lawrence. "Arbitrary Values and Contemporary Music." *New York Times* 15 Apr. 2013, late ed.: A4. *New York Times Ondisc.* CD-ROM.